D1135360

TO:

_____

FROM:

_____

DATE:

_____

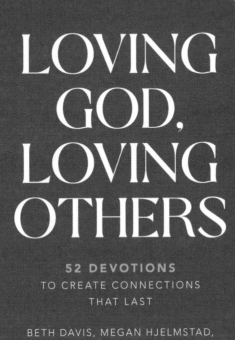

LOVING GOD, LOVING OTHERS

52 DEVOTIONS
TO CREATE CONNECTIONS
THAT LAST

BETH DAVIS, MEGAN HJELMSTAD,
NELL O'LEARY, BONNIE ENGSTROM,
SARAH ERICKSON, AND EMILY STIMPSON CHAPMAN

THOMAS NELSON
Since 1798

This book is dedicated to every woman in the Blessed is
She sisterhood that in our deepened relationship with
Our Lord, we become softer, kinder, and more open to
His grace and peace in every relationship in our lives.

Loving God, Loving Others

© 2022 Blessed is She, Inc.

Published in Nashville, Tennessee, by Thomas Nelson. Thomas Nelson is a registered trademark of HarperCollins Christian Publishing, Inc.

Project director: Jenna Guizar

Project manager and editor, scripture selections and questions: Nell O'Leary, JD

Theological editor: Susanna Spencer, MA in theology

Thomas Nelson titles may be purchased in bulk for educational, business, fund-raising, or sales promotional use. For information, please email SpecialMarkets@ThomasNelson.com.

Scripture quotations are taken from the New Revised Standard Version Bible: Catholic Edition. Copyright © 1989, 1993 National Council of the Churches of Christ in the United States of America. Used by permission. All rights reserved worldwide.

Any internet addresses, phone numbers, or company or product information printed in this book are offered as a resource and are not intended in any way to be or to imply an endorsement by Thomas Nelson, nor does Thomas Nelson vouch for the existence, content, or services of these sites, phone numbers, companies, or products beyond the life of this book.

Cover design and original cover and interior artwork: ash ulmer design

Interior design: Emily Ghattas

ISBN 978-1-4002-3032-7 (audiobook)
ISBN 978-1-4002-3029-7 (eBook)
ISBN 978-1-4002-3028-0 (HC)

Printed in India

22 23 24 25 26 BPI 10 9 8 7 6 5 4 3 2 1

CONTENTS

CONTENTS

INTRODUCTION

BY JENNA GUIZAR

I settle into the couch of a new friend I've made, anxiously wondering if I should be doing something else, sitting somewhere else, acting differently (*How? I don't know!*). I feel the urge to pull out my phone while I wait for her to finish grabbing us a couple of ice waters.

The new friend comes in and sets my water on the table, and we start catching up. As soon as we're talking, trading questions and laughing together about the latest silly moments with our families, I feel my body relax. She is comfortable, safe, kind, and easy to talk to. This new relationship feels easy and peaceful, and I enjoy just chatting with her about nothing and everything.

I ask her about her relationship with the Lord, her prayer life, and her heart. She offers me an answer, one I can respond to with my own experiences, sufferings, joys, consolations, and desolations.

After years of broken friendships and relationships, I'm so grateful the Lord is offering me another one. It doesn't replace the others, of course, but it could bring a fresh outpouring of joy into my life, a renewed sense of friendship and vulnerability—things that have been fractured so painfully before.

I know the Lord is in the business of repairing brokenness, restoring relationships, offering a renewal of laughter and joy in your life too. And it begins with your relationship with Him, with sinking into your own couch with His Word, and with your heart turned toward Him. It begins with stepping into the confessional and saying, "I am coming back to You, Lord," and with going to Mass to receive Jesus, who is and always will be our strength, in the Blessed Sacrament.

Our first and best relationship is with our Faithful Friend, our Lord and Savior. So let's begin there, dear sister. Let us open our hearts once again to Him because He will pour out His love, joy, graces, and friendship. Let Him pour you a glass of Living Water, one that will leave you forever satisfied and wholly loved.

I pray this book will help you enter more deeply into your relationship with the Lord, who is with you and will never leave. The Living Water Himself will comfort you, give you peace, and pour out into all of the relationships in your life.

PART ONE

YOUR RELATIONSHIP WITH GOD

BETH DAVIS

Let us take this time to ask ourselves: *How is my relationship with God, and how have I accepted His invitation to grow in our relationship?*

As we consider this most important relationship, which feeds into all others, we'll walk through eight stories from my life—in contrasting pairs. I'll share a time of distance and closeness in church community, a time of desolation and consolation in prayer, a disconnected and intimate sacramental life, along with dry and fruitful introspection. I encourage you to open your Bible and follow along. Take time with the questions and let them sit inside your heart.

THE LIE OF LONELINESS

DISTANCE AT CHURCH

I took a short, sharp breath and fought back frustrated tears, returning my eyes to the altar. It was my own fault, I supposed. I had arrived late to the earliest morning Mass, and now I couldn't find a seat. I scanned the pews for a single spot, hoping against hope that I could slip into an aisle spot somewhere. After churches reopened from the 2020 pandemic, people were understandably cautious about sitting too near someone outside of their household, much less letting a stranger climb over them to make her way to the middle of a half-empty row.

With no seat in sight, I settled down on the stairs in the back of the church, surrounded by young families. I watched as toddlers toddled and tired parents chased them. Babies cooed and cried as their moms or dads or big siblings bounced and shushed soothingly. From this vantage point, I could see big Catholic families taking up whole pews. And on that particular morning, as I sat alone on those linoleum-lined steps, tears slipped down my cheeks. The full weight of my barrenness as a thirty-seven-year-old single woman sank inside of me.

Seeking to stifle my despair, I tried to reason with myself. I had grown up at this parish. I had fallen in love with Jesus in the adjacent chapel. After my conversion of heart during high school, I had moved away—first to college, then on to an eleven-year career as a youth minister in another city. Finally, all these years later, I had come back to my parish.

But now the space between me and my fellow parishioners was more than a physical divide. A loneliness stirred within me, deeper than sitting alone on the stairs or being single. Even my own precious family and my very best friend couldn't soothe it. I was in a wilderness of the soul, feeling cut off from the joy and connection I observed all around me.

We each have a wilderness in our souls that Christ alone can inhabit. That wilderness could look like infertility, where the desert plains crack your lips with thirst. It might look like grief, where slimy swamp creatures drag you beneath its murky depths. Or maybe it is anxiety, where a jungle of unfamiliar sounds entangles your limbs.

Yet even in the most desolate wilderness, our loneliness is a lie. We are not exiled to those arid places alone, suffering isolation on top of everything else. In the heart of each of our deserts, Christ is there with us.

We encounter this Jesus in this week's scripture: "In the morning, while it was still very dark, he got up and went out to a deserted place, and there he prayed" (Mark 1:35). Jesus, the Light of the

World, knows the wilderness well. He resisted Satan's temptations in the wilderness, and He retreated to deserted places to pray to the Father. He goes ahead of us into our desolation. He meets us there in our prayer.

As I struggled through that morning Mass, feeling completely alone, I wasn't. Jesus had already claimed me at my baptism. He had made His home in me all those years ago. His presence had gone—and still goes—before me to fill every wilderness I had ever walked through and will ever walk through. His love anticipates every moment too painful even for words.

And He is up early to meet you in your wilderness—every wasteland, every swamp, every loss and ache—your whole life long. He is already there, praying for you.

I received Holy Communion that day with tear-streaked cheeks, full of hope that Jesus was already in my wilderness. He is not afraid of the dark in our lives. And if the Light is there waiting, we don't have to be afraid either.

READING: MARK 1:35

- What lie of isolation, loneliness, or forgottenness are you wrestling with? Ask Our Lord to be with you in it.
- If you have felt out of place or are looking for a church community, who reached out to you? To whom can you reach out?

EVEN IN THE
MOST DESOLATE
WILDERNESS,
OUR LONELINESS
IS A LIE.

BETH DAVIS

FINDING CHURCH FAMILY

CLOSENESS AT CHURCH

Oversized grocery carts rattled past as I stood stock-still at the end of the aisle. I had taken his call, pausing my overflowing carts, loaded up with everything we would need to host a women's retreat. The priest on the line was new to me. Save for a few professional emails to talk logistics, we didn't have much of a rapport. When our women's ministry lost our retreat chaplain right before the event, a friend had recommended Father, who offered to help.

On the call, I poured out my gratitude for the gift of his yes to a ministry and team of women he'd never heard of, much less met. In turn, he thanked me for taking a chance on him. He said he knew the risk it took to bring in a pinch hitter in the last inning, and then, with words that stopped me in my tracks, he said, "I want to be as steady as I can for you."

Peace flooded my body. Somebody was on my team. It wasn't all up to me.

For much of my life, I'd been on my own. Not physically, but emotionally and mentally. The stress of trying to hold it all together and the fear of messing it all up had pervaded both my professional and my personal life. Whether running a retreat or in relationships, I lived like an independent and self-protected orphan. Even in prayer, I approached the Lord simply begging for help from a benevolent but busy God, willing to live off the scraps of His attention. I assumed that He too must have limits on His time and care for me.

And I wonder, Have you been believing the same lies? That you're alone in this world? That no one will come along to scoop up your weary bones and hold you? That your burdens are too much for another to bear?

The thing about lies is that they're not true. The Lord isn't a kind stranger or a disinterested passerby. He is not indifferent to your sighs. He is our Father; by our baptism, we are His daughters. And that same Father is the head of a very large family: the Catholic Church.

And you belong.

Here in the Church, you are home, with brothers and sisters more real and more numerous than your biological family. Here, Jesus said in Matthew 18, "where two or three are gathered in my name, I am there among them" (v. 20).

As Father's words washed over me that day, I was drenched in a sense of home. On that phone call, I met family I didn't know existed, and the lonely darkness in my heart was flooded with light. The Lord came to me through a spiritual father, a brother in Christ. And his enduring friendship has proven that original promise true. Father's steady presence has revealed the steadfast love of the Father to me.

But most of all, this holy priest has enfleshed the love of God for me in the Mass, calling down the Holy Spirit to miraculously change ordinary bread and wine into Jesus' Precious Body and Blood. That's how badly Jesus wants us to know that we're not alone: He comes to live inside of us, to become one flesh with us, and to make us one with one another. With the Lord, we enjoy a banquet before us in the Church—in the bread that becomes His Body and the people beside us at the table.

In God's abundance, He's given us both a place and people to remind us we aren't alone. So when those lies hiss convincingly, go to the Church; run to God's people. There you'll find Him in your midst.

READING: MATTHEW 18:20

- Who has enfleshed God's love for you? Maybe you are called to be that person for someone else. Who would that be?
- God designed us to thrive in community. Consider small steps to build a more intentional community today. What might those steps be?

WHEN GOD IS SILENT

PRAYER DESOLATION

I stood under the dim streetlamp, staring at my phone. Flight canceled. Not rescheduled. Canceled. I stuttered my excuses to a disinterested Lyft driver, closed the backseat door, and steered my luggage back toward the house, tears forming in the corners of my eyes.

What was I supposed to do in the middle of the night?

I should have been preparing to board a cross-country red-eye flight to make the Ignatian silent retreat of my dreams. Eight blissful days of peace and intimacy with Jesus, the Lover of my soul, alongside sweet religious sisters.

As I frantically dialed the airline and explained my dilemma, I felt abandoned by God, the very One I ached to be with. *Why are You allowing this, Lord? All I want is to be with You. Why is this so hard?*

Even though I was able to rebook my flight, I would no longer be there in time to meet the other sisters or be present for the opening Mass. I would not get to enjoy dinner with my spiritual director or spend a day exploring the grounds before entering into nearly a week's worth of silence.

And when I finally did arrive at the sleepy retreat house after a long, lonely, sleepless night and a brutal day of travel, I collapsed on the stiff mattress and let out a barking cough, knowing that for the next eight days my lungs would burn and my body would ache. But the missed flight and respiratory troubles were just the beginning, and the least painful part, of that week.

I had anticipated quiet on the grounds of the retreat center and in the chapel, but I did not expect silence from God. For eight days, I encountered only a cold and vast silence. I felt my cries echo off canyon walls and return to me as desperate as they had left my lips. I tried, but I couldn't reach across the void. *Where are You, God? Why can't I hear You or feel You here?*

The longing that drove me to seek God in that retreat house's unfamiliar chapel seemed to mock me as I strained to hear something. Why would He give me this desire to fly with Him only to leave me standing alone on the edge of something beautiful? Why is God sometimes silent? Where are His words when our souls cry out to Him and the loneliness presses out all the air from our lungs? How can the Father seem the farthest from us when we are grasping for a hand?

Perhaps you have stood on this edge. Desperate for help in a financial crisis, aching for comfort after a breakup, reaching out for some sense of stability after a diagnosis—and instead you were left feeling empty-handed.

In those lonely hours, our voices do not go unheard. No, they are joined with another voice that cried out to our hearing, yet hidden, Father: "My God, my God, why have you forsaken me?" (Matthew 27:46). From the cross, Jesus gasped these words of the psalmist, forever joining the chorus of hearts that shout out to God. When we stand overlooking this chasm—when we seek God but hear silence—we do not stand alone. Jesus' outstretched arms reach back. His prayer answers ours. His heart covers the distance.

During those eight nights, sleep and oxygen eluded me, but He was there. In the quiet hours on that hard pew, He listened to everything I said and failed to say. He gave me space. When I wept alone before His stone form hanging from the crumbling cross, He looked back at me. His knowing eyes were full of love and suffering—with me, for me.

The Lord is not unmoved by your efforts to seek Him in prayer. He is not deaf to your cries in the midnight hours. He does not turn His back when tears slip down your face. When you fear you will never hear Him again, instead breathe deeply.

Even the silence is filled with Him.

READING: MATTHEW 27:46

- Even silence is filled with God's presence. Meditate on this truth.
- What do you take to Jesus over and over again in prayer? Remind yourself that He is listening even when it feels as though He is not.

EVEN THE
SILENCE IS FILLED
WITH GOD.

BETH DAVIS

HIS GIFT OF ORANGES

PRAYER CONSOLATION

I whipped the car around at the flash of orange and parked in front of a stranger's house. Cautiously, I approached the cardboard box, its floppy sides advertising "free" in black letters, and stood open-mouthed in disbelief. The very citrus fruit I'd been praying for lay picked and piled before me, in grocery bags and everything.

It was a simple, neighborly gesture—leaving a box of excess produce on the sidewalk—but it may as well have been a flashing neon sign. *God is faithful.* That's what these oranges beamed.

You see, every Lent I would ask the Lord what He wanted me to do. Instead of diving headlong into whatever I thought I needed to conquer, I would pray and listen for God's voice. I stood before that unfamiliar house, half laughing, half crying at the overflowing oranges in answer to my Lenten prayer. When I had asked God what He wanted me to do (or not do), I couldn't get away from the idea that I should eat an orange every day.

Bananas, I remember thinking (no pun intended).

So I had run it by a priest, mentioned it to a few prayerful friends, and kept asking God what He wanted from me because, surely, this wasn't it.

And yet, the answer was always the same: eat an orange every day. So, on Ash Wednesday, the Holy Spirit and I had set out for Trader Joe's. But as I'd picked out my first penitential bag of clementines, all my peace had evaporated.

I was right about the oranges, but wrong about having to buy or pick them. On the drive home from the grocery store, I had felt the Lord ask me to open my hand and receive, to let Him provide for me instead of taking care of myself. And the peace had returned.

That Lent, I developed a heightened sensitivity to the color orange, to friends' fruit bowls, to the abundant citrus trees lining Arizona roads, willing one of its fruits into my hands. All the while, fear and insecurity chattered away: *Where will my orange come from today? Does He really care about giving me a silly orange? Does He really care about* me?

As the Lenten season unfolded before me, what had begun as painful prying became joyful expectation. Day by day, orange by orange, I was surprised to find that He would always fill my shaking hands. With every juicy bite, I tasted the sweetness of a God who provides.

Maybe you're wondering, too, if the Lord really cares. Does He care that you're overlooked at work or that your loved one's memory is getting worse? Does He hear your prayers for a new home or a good, holy spouse? Will He provide for that student loan payment or the desires of your heart?

I can assure you that He does and He will. Because every day of that Lent, the Lord answered my questions with an orange.

In the Gospel of Saint John, Jesus promised, "So you have pain now; but I will see you again, and your hearts will rejoice, and no one will take your joy from you" (16:22). With each orange, He took my fear, my doubt, my striving—all the pain of not knowing if God truly cared and would provide—and turned them into joy.

I could have bought a week's supply of produce at the store or picked a bunch from my neighbor's tree. I could have provided for myself. But I would have missed the invitation into intimacy. I would have missed the heart of the Father, who wants to give good gifts to His children.

Our Lord is still speaking, still working, still giving. And friend, I don't want you to miss it either.

READING: JOHN 16:22

- How are you trusting God to provide for you right now, and how is He doing so?
- Consider the times of consolation in prayer. What did they feel like, sound like? Now hold them close during the rough patches.

A FRESH START

DISCONNECTED SACRAMENTAL LIFE

The beautiful purple satin stole hung around his neck in stark contrast to our rustic surroundings. Father was on his way to his car when I surprised him in the dirt parking lot of our Newman Center by asking to go to confession, but he graciously made time. Deftly, he drew out the liturgical garment from his pocket, and we sat together in the sunshine of the parking lot.

After making the sign of the cross, I sighed heavily and began, "Bless me, Father, for I have sinned. It's been two months since my last confession." Once again, I found myself reciting the same tired sins, only this time to a different priest. I rattled my way through, avoiding eye contact with the many passersby. When I ended my confession, the gentle priest didn't scold or shame me, but instead offered me some heartfelt advice.

He wisely encouraged me to come back to confession—and soon. Father shared that his own experience of the sacrament had become even more powerful and fruitful with regular reception of reconciliation. If I wanted to make greater strides in love and holiness, he recommended staying connected to Jesus by receiving the abundant grace available in the sacrament every two weeks.

Indeed, I had been struggling through those past few months without making much progress. Try as I might to rid myself of my sharp tongue and laziness (to name a couple), I couldn't. I wondered if I would ever become the woman I knew God was calling me to be, the woman I truly desired to be. But as my sins stacked up, I felt farther and farther away from being her.

Perhaps you also have a vision of yourself, a perfect picture of the put-together version of you. Fit and polished, gracious and accomplished, with an immaculate house and a happy family. You might even get close to being her some days. But other days, maybe more frequently than you'd like to admit, you snap at the people you love most, you avoid or resent the hard work of sacrificial love, and you fall into bed restless and regretful.

On days like those, when accusation rings in my ears and sin weighs heavy on my soul, Father's words press through the rocky soil to grow and bloom once more in my heart. The hope of forgiveness, a fresh start, and supernatural grace beckons me to return to the sacrament.

Jesus bids us come because He is not surprised by our weakness or failures. He knows how incapable we are of doing anything without Him. "Abide in me as I abide in you," Jesus said in Saint John's Gospel. "Just as the branch cannot bear fruit by itself unless it abides in the vine, neither can you unless you abide in me" (15:4).

We are little branches, but we are capable of bearing so much fruit if only we stay connected to Him. Jesus supplies everything we need, strengthening us from within, pumping His very life into us as we stay close to Him. This is truly the Good News: We are not alone. We don't have to do anything alone.

As the warm afternoon sun shone over us, the priest lifted his hands to absolve me of my sins, and the lifeblood of Our Precious Savior once more flowed unobstructed through my soul. That same healing and saving power is available for you. Jesus' forgiveness will restore health to the rot and decay within you. His love and Spirit will make your little efforts fruitful. And suddenly—through Him and with Him and in Him—you'll find that your life has borne an orchard full of good fruit.

READING: JOHN 15:4

- Do you have a spiritual-health routine that includes regular confession? If not, get it on the calendar.
- Jesus brings health and healing and guidance for better habits. Which habits do you want to leave behind today? What new habits will replace them?

THIS IS TRULY
THE GOOD NEWS:
WE ARE NOT
ALONE.

BETH DAVIS

FORGIVE YOURSELF

INTIMATE SACRAMENTAL LIFE

The priest scanned the crowd sincerely before fixing his eyes on me in the pew. "Forgive yourself," he said simply. Unable to return his kind and determined gaze, I lifted my tear-filled eyes to the crucifix.

I had been warming the pews of Holy Spirit Parish every single morning at Mass for the better part of a year. The constancy of my mostly elderly fellow worshippers and the rhythm of the liturgy became an anchor in my every day.

Each morning, I was drawn into the current of the ancient and universal prayer of the Church, steadied by the familiar movement of the Mass. But during those months in which I had sat and stood and knelt, I noticed something loosening from deep within and bubbling up to the surface.

Old and painful memories, the relics of past sexual sin, floated up before my eyes. I felt shame's dark and unwelcome presence in my too-big body as I uncomfortably tugged at my clothes. And every morning at eight, I found myself distracted by all the ways I'd failed the day before, and last week, and a lifetime ago.

Shame, I discovered, had been my constant companion.

I had tried for years to dispel the darkness. Frequenting the sacrament of confession, committing to a diet and exercise plan (again), trying harder tomorrow. And the Lord was generous to heal and save me.

In the sacraments, He set me free from sin, His grace rescuing me out of unhealthy relationships. In His Word, He told me I was beautiful and loved. In personal prayer, He buoyed me with His patience and compassion.

Still, shame overwhelmed me, miring me in its muddy depths. Despite the Savior's inexhaustible mercy, I couldn't forgive myself.

I began to hear the invitation in my heart. The gentle voice seemed to touch every part of me: *Forgive yourself.* When a memory flooded me in the middle of the night, *Forgive yourself.* As I walked out of the confessional, *Forgive yourself.* When I made a mistake at work or with a friend, *Forgive yourself.* And then again, from the fatherly priest with the heart of the Father—*Forgive yourself.*

Those words are for you too.

Let them wash over you when your wounds torment you and the pain of thinking it's all your fault washes over you. After you've unburdened your heart in confession, forgive yourself.

Jesus suffered and died and rose again so that we wouldn't suffocate under the weight of our own sin and shame. Even now, He comes alongside us, first to share, then to lift, and finally to take our burdens upon Him.

Our Merciful Lord saw me sitting in the pew that morning and at every Mass before then. He heard my midnight prayers and received my tears in every confession. So when my memory wouldn't let me forget, when the weight loss wasn't working, or when the next day I was the same me I had been the day before, Jesus whispered, "I will not leave you orphaned; I am coming to you" (John 14:18).

This Jesus has never left you. He will never leave you. And His love and mercy are coming for you just as they came for me when He pursued me in that seemingly unremarkable morning Mass.

As I raised my eyes to the cross, wiping away tears to see His sweet face, I heard the tender words of my pastor. They echoed in my soul. The Savior wasn't content to watch me suffer when He had already suffered for me. *Forgive yourself.*

READING: JOHN 14:18–19

- Do you tend to hold on to self-loathing or condemnation? Bring it to Jesus in prayer today.
- How can you answer this encouraging (yet difficult) call to forgive yourself? Is this something you want to explore with a friend or loved one in conversation?

WEEK 7

GOD ALONE SATISFIES

THIRST UNMET

I shifted my weight nervously and pressed a hand to my flaming cheeks. Though not a terribly long line, the wait to receive the sacrament of confession seemed excruciating. I tried to read the examination of conscience, dug around in my soul and memory for what to confess, but one sin dominated my teenage years: pornography.

I'd been there before, fidgety and red-faced, anxious to confess the sins of impurity that I'd committed . . . again. Month after month, I had darkened the doors of a dozen churches, head hanging low, aching to be free from the guilt, only to fall again a few days or weeks later and feel the shame descend anew.

For years I had fought against those disordered affections, and mostly alone. Outside of the confessional, I felt too embarrassed to share my struggles with anyone. My friends all seemed so normal and carefree, happy and at ease in real relationships with their high

23

school boyfriends. I'd never been in a relationship—never even been kissed—and yet I'd seen and done and fantasized about all kinds of sexual behavior.

But the longing for connection and intimacy was so deep, the images and the reward they brought so irresistible, that I couldn't stop. Porn promised me an escape and a release from the loneliness of my home and the insecurity about my body, and a taste of the closeness I ached for without the risk of rejection. At times, my thirst was so all-consuming that it pushed out every other thought. Longing for a drink, I turned to the counterfeit fountain of lust and drank deeply. But in the wake of my indulgence, I found myself even more parched than before.

Exhausted and discouraged in this spiritual desert, I would drag myself across the sands of shame to stand once more in that slow-moving confessional line. In all of those confessionals over those many years, I sought to cleanse my soul and palate from the poison of pornography. In faith, I knew that the grace of the sacrament of confession flowed over every dry place, but with little support and long-lived habits, my progress was almost imperceptible.

When your own efforts to grow in holiness and to stop sinning fall short, when your strength is weak and you're tempted to think things will never change, don't despair. Don't lose hope. The One who satisfies the deepest desires of the human heart understands your pain. He Himself entered into and endured it.

In the Gospel of Saint John, in Jesus' last agonizing moments, He said something we might expect but which means more than we could even hope for: "I am thirsty" (19:28). He wasn't only speaking of physical thirst; He was expressing His urgent desire for the love of every human heart—including yours. On the cross, Jesus descended to meet us in our shame and isolation. And it is there, in the loneliest of places, that we find our thirst is drowned in the immense love of His own Sacred Heart.

We drink of this love in the sacraments and in personal prayer where Jesus, the Living Water, washes over our sins, saturates our deepest desire for connection and understanding, and satisfies our insatiable thirst for perfect love.

After years of returning to Him in confession, crying out for healing, and pouring out my heart to the Lord, His mercy finally broke through, and I was completely healed and delivered from lust, pornography, and masturbation.

Praise God from whom all blessings flow.

Sister, give Him your heart. Quench His thirst for you, every single day. And no matter how long it takes, He will quench your thirst and satisfy your longings too. He's the only One who can.

READING: JOHN 19:28

- Where do you desire God, the Living Water, to wash over you? Have you brought this desire to the sacrament of confession? Is there a particular sin cycle in your life that you haven't been able to break?
- If you're facing discouragement, reach out in trust to the Blessed Virgin Mary and ask her to intercede on your behalf.

OUR THIRST IS
DROWNED IN THE
IMMENSE LOVE OF
HIS OWN SACRED
HEART.

BETH DAVIS

FEAST ON HIM

HUNGER FULFILLED

My eyes shot open in the dark hours of the morning, heart pounding, scripture verses resonating in my mind. Pentecost was today, and the Holy Spirit was in the room. I had fallen asleep with tears on my cheeks. I had not felt or heard God in prayer in weeks. He was hidden from me. In those quiet months since the pandemic of 2020 had begun, we were all separated from the Lord's presence in the sacraments. I couldn't receive Him in Mass or visit Him in the chapel. Despite my hardworking faith, I couldn't muscle my way through.

I had prayed in all my favorite ways, had read beloved passages in Scripture, had talked to my spiritual director, all to no avail. Without the comfort and constancy of the sacraments, my nerves were stretched thin. I ached for God. As I had lain in bed, weeping, I had poured out my longing to feel His presence and love until I finally had fallen asleep, empty and exhausted.

The isolation in those early days that stretched into weeks and months had brought with it a gnawing hunger for peace, for the people I loved most, and for the normal life I longed to live. Instead, I had to survive on scraps.

Can you relate to this distance or the ache for God? Have you been living off the vestiges of childhood faith and settling for the cultural religion of your family, never embracing an intimate and personal relationship with the Savior? Are you frustrated and lonely, reciting rote prayers, but never truly connecting with God? Or have you been away from the sacraments for too long, having fallen out of the habit?

Sister, our souls will starve if our faith stays shallow, and they will die if we turn to the fast food of the world to satisfy our hunger. On another table, the Eucharist table, Jesus lays a feast before us and welcomes us to come and eat—with Him, of Him.

Restless, I had fallen asleep with an ache in my belly, but on the anniversary of the coming of the Holy Spirit, He came. He nourished me. He brought me back to life. The Lord's voice rang through the silence in scripture verses leaping into my imagination, ones I didn't know I knew, painting lush pictures that made sense of my heart and calling. Answers to questions I didn't know I had were spread before me like a banquet, which I feasted on. But above all, I feasted on the closeness of God's presence.

I savor these words and images from my Pentecost visitation. I can still feel God's presence, still taste the peace He brought with Him. Those sleepless hours were full of the love and connection I craved, and they feed me to this day.

In Saint Matthew's Gospel, Jesus promised, "Blessed are those who hunger and thirst for righteousness, for they will be filled" (5:6). That emptiness in your heart can be filled. It *will* be filled by the very One who created it.

If you hunger, He will fill you. That is the promise.

So if you're hungry, come to Jesus. If you're longing for true food and real presence, cry out to Him. If you're tired of a life of drive-thru substitutes leaving you sick and dissatisfied, hold out your hands, and He will fill them with good things, with Himself. He will send you His Holy Spirit to renew your flagging spirit and strengthen your weak body. He will nurse you back to health.

This life of abundance is for you. A nourishing life of prayer is for you, because even more than you desire Him, dear sister, He desires you.

READING: MATTHEW 5:6

- Quietly examine your prayer life. Are you nourished? What is the hunger you want Jesus to fill right now?
- Our God wants to be close to us. Consider how frequently you receive the Blessed Sacrament and how frequently you go to confession. Is there room for allowing Him to draw closer to you through more frequent visits to the sacraments?

PART TWO

YOUR
RELATIONSHIP
WITH YOURSELF

MEGAN HJELMSTAD

Let us take this time to ask ourselves: *How do I relate to myself as made in God's image and likeness?*

In this section, we'll walk through eight stories from my life—in contrasting pairs—to examine the way we understand and know ourselves as women of God. I'll share discouragement with and confidence in my personal appearance, perceived flaws and a belief in my gifts and abilities, a challenging and a joyful relationship with food, and feeling trapped in a life path and taking a leap of faith. I encourage you to open your Bible and follow along. Take time with the questions and let them sit inside your heart.

HUNGRY FOR ACCEPTANCE

DISCOURAGEMENT IN APPEARANCE

I had just finished my Army contract, moved across the country, and begun my long-desired role as a stay-at-home mom. After years of eighteen-hour workdays, obediently following orders, and giving commands, I could finally be with my kids full-time. However, I quickly discovered I had traded a unit of obedient soldiers who followed my every order for toddlers who needed me nonstop and who defied my every direction. By the end of the first week, I was drowning in a sea of boxes and overwhelming demands.

In desperation, I fled to story time at the library, where I struck up a conversation with a fellow mom. When she invited me to the playground with a few other moms who were new to the area, relief washed over me. But the more I got to know these new friends, the more I noticed our differing values. Their conversations centered around high-end baby gear, luxury vehicles, and designer labels.

I had spent nine years in uniform. While I enjoyed nice things, I suddenly felt like a misfit.

It came to a head one day as a mom shared that she'd taken her baby to get his first pair of TOMS. "What are TOMS?" I blurted out, regretting it immediately. The other moms exchanged raised eyebrows; I quietly melted in shame. From that moment forward, I scoured the internet for designer clothes I couldn't afford in an attempt to fit in. Even as these so-called friends eventually moved away and I developed a healthier, faith-based community, I could always find someone better dressed or more affluent.

While my faith remained a lifeline, I allowed the truth of my God-given identity to become buried under a desire for superficial acceptance. The temptation was all around me and kept me scrambling to possess enough to be accepted. Yet in all my spinning, I never seemed to acquire enough or feel as if I were enough.

Exhausted from the charade, I brought my struggle to the Lord. I knew intellectually that God loved me—yet it was only when I started to spend time in relationship with Him that I experienced this truth. My openness allowed Him the much-needed time and space to teach me about my identity as His beloved daughter.

Through prayer, God slowly revealed that my craving for worldly acceptance had been rooted in old wounds, some reaching back to my childhood. I came to understand that my fear of rejection stemmed from a deeper fear that I was not good—and was therefore *unlovable.*

God's voice broke through the fear, not in accusation, but in invitation: "Why do you worry about clothing?" (Matthew 6:28). God was not exasperated by my struggle; He wanted me to let Him into it. What was once a guilt-laden fight against the temptation of materialism became a doorway to His healing.

When I finally gave God access to the tender parts of my heart, He could teach me how to live out my true identity, allowing His love to clothe me in His incomparable glory.

Sometimes, we fear that if someone discovers who we are, that person won't love us. You might be tempted to trade the dignity of God's love for superficial admiration, or believe that hiding your authentic identity from the world will protect you. Yet, as I discovered, distorting your identity to appease worldly expectations only brings more pain. Your worth does not lie in wishing away your unique identity, but rather in embracing it.

God loves us for who we already are, people made in His image and likeness. When we bring Him our struggles, He heals our identity so we do not have to needlessly spin to seek our worth—but can instead allow Him to clothe us in the glory of our authentic selves.

READING: MATTHEW 6:28–29

- Have you felt judged or trapped by the perception other people have of you? Let God breathe some freedom into this now.
- If rejection is part of your life story, examine those feelings. Now think through any instances where you may have rejected others. How can you move forward with an open, vulnerable, and inclusive heart?

GIVE THE LORD
ACCESS TO THE
TENDER PARTS OF
YOUR HEART.

MEGAN HJELMSTAD

MOVING PAST MY IMPERFECTIONS

CONFIDENCE IN APPEARANCE

"All for You, Lord, whatever the outcome," I prayed silently as I stepped up to the podium for my keynote speech, the usual flutters of anticipation followed by a surprising wave of excitement. The talk flew by with ease, and afterward, a smiling woman approached me, her face aglow.

"Thank you so much!" she gushed. "You speak so effortlessly! So many practical tips too!"

I had invested hours of prep time in prayer, begging for the Holy Spirit's guidance and surrendering the end result to Him. I blushed as she spoke, my spirit filled with awe and my heart swelling with gratitude at God's grace in this moment. I was both humbled and exhilarated, considering the long road that had brought me here.

Growing up, I was the shy kid. I barely spoke two words in kindergarten and stood motionless with stage fright during my first Girl Scout troop performance. I both dreaded and stumbled through school presentations. My most humiliating memories were (unsurprisingly) tied directly to public speaking. How could I forget the wide eyes and the extended, diplomatic silence that followed an unrehearsed briefing I had to deliver at my first military assignment?

Later, my love of writing took off, reinforcing my belief that my voice was best confined to the written form. "I'm a writer because I write far better than I speak!" I would quip in conversation.

I truly believed that I was too inarticulate and lacking in necessary confidence to speak well. I listened raptly to professional speakers and marveled. Becoming a professional speaker myself seemed as impossible as sprouting wings and taking flight.

No one was more surprised than I was when the Lord started dropping public speaking opportunities at my doorstep. The over-arching draw was that in every instance, I got to talk about *Him*. It began as uncomfortable, exhausting work. I wrote out every talk verbatim and practiced for hours to make it sound conversational, not robotic. Even as I gained confidence and came prepared with mere outlines, old wounds and doubts still plagued me. I'd rehash every imperfection, despite the positive feedback I received.

They're probably trying to make me feel better. I'm just a writer.

Yet I couldn't argue with the evidence: the invitations kept coming, and I started getting invited back—to the same places—to speak again.

What I had deemed unthinkable, God had been making possible all along. He created something out of nothing, not because I was secretly so great—but rather, so His greatness could be made manifest through me. My weakness became a testimony to the power of His strength.

Fear had blinded me to the gift God had given me to reflect His image to the world. Relying solely on my own power restricted His freedom to make the "impossible" possible (see Matthew 19:26). Yet when I stepped outside my comfort zone into His will, He made incredible things happen.

If you're facing a seemingly impossible situation, remember that the Enemy concentrates his fiercest attacks on your greatest areas of potential. Satan trembles at the areas you perceive as impossibilities because out of these God brings redemption.

Of course, obedience to God isn't a magic wand to grant our every wish; rather, *He* will perfect and make possible what He desires. He gives us both visible and hidden gifts to make a great impact on the world, not for our own egos, but for His glory, our sanctity, and the eternal building of His Kingdom.

Let us dare to bring our impossibilities to God and be amazed at the results.

READING: MATTHEW 19:26

- Are you struggling to figure out what gifts God has given you? Pay attention and keep following where He is leading you.
- Your weakness is made perfect in His strength, so if you are self-conscious about weaknesses, offer them to God. What does that sound like?

DISSECTING EVERY INTERACTION

PERCEIVED FLAWS

"Happy birthday to you. . . ."

The lights dimmed and our discordant voices joined with enthusiasm as my fiancé looked up in surprise. I had secretly traveled to his ski competition and organized the whole team for a birthday dinner. My fiancé's surprise gave way to a grin as he caught sight of me carrying the cake I had decorated.

As the singing faded, I went to grab some plates, then heard a burst of laughter coming from the table. "They spelled 'Happy Birthday' wrong!" My fiancé pointed at the letters on the cake that I'd inadvertently switched. I froze, horrified.

He clearly had no idea I'd decorated it, but one glance at my face, and he realized his blunder. He slipped away from the group and began to apologize profusely, while I tried to casually play it off.

Inside, however, I was already berating myself. *I'm about to graduate from one of the top schools in the country, and I can't even spell! How dumb can I be?*

This internal, self-accusing script was nothing new. It had been a toxic companion since my childhood, and the burden of perfectionism had only mounted as pressure increased to do well in school, gain acceptance, and boast a résumé of accomplishments. This perfectionism had even wormed its way deep into ministry work and my personal faith life. I would catch myself replaying every conversation or picking apart every word to evaluate whether it was good enough—and more important, whether *I* was.

The more I cared about a particular person's approval, the more I dissected our interaction. *Did I get it right? Does he respect me? Is she being nice on the surface but secretly judging me?* I constantly assured others that their worth was based in God, not accomplishments or acceptance, but I couldn't manage to accept this wisdom for myself. My own wounds of rejection ran so deep that I needed to do everything perfectly to garner others' approval and be considered "good."

The more time I spent rehashing my words and actions, the more room Satan had to convince me that I was a failure, a reject, and *not* good. I felt I had to work harder, be more perfect, and change myself in countless ways to earn acceptance and worth.

I related this struggle to my spiritual director one day, and she responded, "You know, Jesus is the only person who ever said or did things perfectly." In that moment, I realized that even absolute perfection didn't save Our Lord from pain and rejection.

As I took this insight to prayer, it became clear that expending all my energy trying to "store up" these worldly treasures would only lead to greater spiritual poverty (see Matthew 6:19–21). I was making an idol out of unattainable worldly perfection, chasing temporary things and imperfect people, who could never have the power to affirm my worth. In reality, only God has the power to save me and help me discover my true, irrevocable dignity.

Do you find yourself getting caught up in perfectionism or worrying about other imperfect people's opinions more than seeking God's? If we try to do everything perfectly, hardly anything will ever get done, and other people's affirmation will never be enough.

Yet when we seek faithfulness above perfectionism, God blesses our imperfect efforts and perfects what He needs to for the sake of His Kingdom. The key is trying our best to be obedient to Him. Whether we succeed or fail by worldly standards, we'll be storing up heavenly treasures that will enrich our hearts and lives—now and into eternity.

READING: MATTHEW 6:19–21

- Does perfectionism factor into your pursuits and insecurities? Set it aside to focus on how God blesses our imperfections.
- What earthly treasures are you tempted to store up? Popularity? Money? Praise? Replace them with the heavenly treasure of seeking to do God's will.

ONLY THE LORD
HAS THE POWER
TO SAVE ME.

MEGAN HJELMSTAD

BELIEF IN MYSELF

GIFTS AND ABILITIES

"You need a backup plan." My high school counselor slid the application across the desk. "You won't get into West Point or any other service academy with these grades and SAT scores. Maybe try other colleges?" I collected the packet and offered a cursory "thank you" as I made a quick exit. His proclamation ignited a tiny fire of defiance in me.

I had just started my senior year of high school and felt I was destined for a service academy. I had taken prep classes to significantly raise my standardized test scores, completed early applications, and met with the springboard diving coaches at three separate academies all now actively recruiting me. I certainly wasn't a star, just reasonably strong in academics, sports, and a slew of experiences that presented a convincing case. That and deep down, I believed that God was calling me to West Point.

So I plowed ahead in determination. When I made my student visit to West Point that October, the coach shocked me on my last day of the trip with an early offer of admission. Offers from the Air Force and Naval Academies followed within days. Thrilled and a bit smug, I marched into my counselor's office to display the offers.

My counselor had set realistic expectations to save me the pain of dashed dreams. What he couldn't see, however, was my God-given potential. God had planted and begun cultivating the gifts deep within me—gifts He desired to grow through His life path for me if I was brave enough to say yes.

As I started down the path of military leadership, I saw how the Lord intended to use these gifts for others' good and His glory. Through my limitations, the Lord was able to grow my humility to become the servant leader He had created me to be. Since I couldn't rely wholly on myself, I leaned on God's supernatural resources.

Though it was a challenge, and though I didn't have as much tactical expertise as my peers, I had a particular set of gifts no one else did. I knew personally how the military environment routinely stripped soldiers of human dignity. As I rose in rank, I worked to build genuine relationships and affirm the dignity of every team member. As soldiers sought me out for advice, I began to understand why God would ask someone like me to do a job like this. I was different; I approached my field with a heart and an intellect that were scarce in our profession.

Nearly twenty years after I received that unlikely service academy acceptance letter, I opened an email message from one of my soldiers. It shared all the ways my leadership characteristics had helped him during our assignment together. It was heaps more than I'd ever realized; tears of gratitude streamed down my face. God had allowed me to be a light in the darkness and make an impact in ways I never expected because I had leaned into the gifts and abilities He'd given me.

The Lord invites us into His work, not because He needs us, but because He truly wants to share it with us. At times you might be tempted to believe there's no room for what you have to offer in a seemingly saturated world. Yet no one can impact the same circle of people you can. No one else has the same life experiences that you do. Your particular gifts are the way God manifests His love to those who might never encounter it otherwise.

When we believe our light—our unique, God-given gifts and insight—isn't important, our corner of the world goes dark. Yet when we embrace our gifts, we shine with God's goodness from the inside out and light up the night. So "let your light shine" to bring all the glory to God (Matthew 5:16).

READING: MATTHEW 5:16

- Think about someone who didn't believe in you and someone who did. Forgive the former and offer prayers of thanksgiving for the latter. What is God doing in your heart?
- What light do you bring to a room? It may be hard to put your finger on it, but it is unique to you. Ask the Holy Spirit to help you find that light and shine it more brightly.

ISOLATION IN MY BODY

CHALLENGE WITH FOOD

"Wow! You look fantastic!" crowed my former roommate as I squealed and swooped in for a hug. We hadn't seen each other since college and were finally reunited for her wedding. We had met years earlier at West Point, and when we weren't studying or cooking up shenanigans in our room, we had stayed busy with our respective sports. At that time I was at the peak of my athletic acumen, but things had changed a bit since then.

Now, as I heaved my suitcase from the car, she stood back to appraise my bony frame, persisting in a string of compliments. "Thanks," I ventured with an outward smile, while grimacing internally. My notably slim body, seemingly flawless to her, was in reality starved for nutrition. The superficial side of me reveled in the praise; the rest of me ached to tell her how unhealthy I really was.

In recent years, I had been plagued by increasing chronic health issues, and the foods my body accepted had dwindled to a pitifully short list as doctors shrugged in bewilderment. This was certainly the skinniest I'd ever been in my adult life, a covetous thing by the world's standards—yet I was the most unwell I had ever been.

I felt isolated, as so many social interactions were centered around food, and the isolation was compounded by the contradicting worldly message that my gauntness was actually good. The sicker I got, the more I realized how unhealthy modern society's perception of beauty is. I had been in my optimal physical condition when I had weighed the most, yet our culture's perspective applauded my scrawny thinness.

As the praise continued and increasingly flattered me, I craved staying painfully skinny almost as much as I craved real food. Despite countless doctor appointments for my health issues, I worried that I might gain back some (much-needed!) weight if I did recover. Things came to a head one day as I looked back at college photos and cringed. I savagely picked apart every detail in pictures I had once loved: *Ugh. Look how fat my face was. Why did I ever like this picture of me?*

My physical sickness had translated into a mental and spiritual sickness, parading in front of me a distorted view of truth, beauty, and goodness. In feeding myself the Enemy's lies, I had corrupted not only my picture of real health but my understanding of my true identity in Christ.

It was God's Word that pulled me out of the spiral of self-criticism and self-deception. Scripture never once describes Christ's personal appearance or the size and shape of the saints. Holiness doesn't hinge upon those things. Holiness is about how we receive the Lord and seek to do His will.

LOVING GOD, LOVING OTHERS

The Enemy tries to distract us with unhealthy relationships with food and fitness. But the Lord knows what we often forget: we cannot "live by bread alone," and we will only achieve lasting health by feeding continually on "every word that comes from the mouth of God" (Matthew 4:4).

If you're feeling famished after consuming the culture's lies, feed on Christ. Run to the Eucharist in Mass and Adoration. Seek out the healing sacrament of confession. Crack open Holy Scripture. The Lord intimately understands our hunger; He became Man specifically to answer our hunger with Himself.

Where earthly food satisfies only briefly, Christ offers His very Body, the Bread of Life, as everlasting fulfillment. When feasts of worldly lies only lead to greater sickness, feeding on God's Word brings soul-deep health and healing. Let us seek God first that we might truly live with bodies made in His likeness.

READING: MATTHEW 4:4

- Does concern over your physical size and appearance consume you? How does meditating on the truth of your identity in Christ help you?
- Is reading Scripture already a part of your prayer routine? How could you implement more disciplined time with the Lord in His Word? Do you feel fed by Him?

GOD BECAME MAN
TO ANSWER OUR
HUNGER WITH
HIMSELF.

MEGAN HJELMSTAD

THAT GRILLED DELIGHT

JOY WITH FOOD

It all started with a grilled cheese sandwich.

It was lunchtime, and my teenage daughter stood watchfully over a sizzling pan, coaxing the crust of her grilled cheese to turn a perfect golden brown. My mouth watered at the aroma. "You really have to try grilled cheese and tomato one of these days!" I declared. My daughter raised an eyebrow. "I promise it's better than it sounds," I laughed, drifting into nostalgia as I recounted a favorite memory.

I had landed my first job as a young teen at the local swim club and was working in the snack shack. The modest shack also had a grill run by an under-celebrated cook. Among the usual suspects of burgers, hot dogs, and pizza, her menu included a signature dish: grilled cheese with tomato. I spent countless afternoons savoring bites of crisped bread layered with slices of juicy beefsteak tomatoes and oozing with white cheese.

Back in my own kitchen, I swallowed the familiar wave of sadness. It had been years since I'd savored anything close to grilled
cheese. Chronic health issues had severely reduced my diet; I
doubted whether I would ever relish the taste of grilled cheese and
tomato again—or countless other foods, for that matter.

I pushed back this same grief every holiday as our families
gathered for meals, every time friends planned an outing around
food or drinks, every time travel came up. I always had to bring my
own food to gatherings to avoid serious sickness. I could never safely
order from a restaurant. Traveling required access to a full kitchen,
grocery shopping and cooking, and packing meals for flights. It
was exhausting, including the continual grief over foods I missed
and pity from others.

Yet as I recounted my memory to my daughter, inspiration
struck. *What if I made it for her?* That very afternoon, I set out to
the grocery store for fresh bread, juicy tomatoes, soft butter, and
cheese. Soon my family was sitting down to their very first grilled
cheese with tomato, and they were instant converts.

What a powerful lesson in the midst of suffering: even if I could
no longer enjoy my favorite things, I could still pass on that enjoy-
ment. The next Christmas, I loaded my kids' stockings with Nutella,
just like I'd received as a kid. At Easter time, they discovered the
Ferrero Rocher chocolates that had been my most beloved treat.

A shift occurred in me. Rather than harboring resentment and
mourning unfulfilled longings, I discovered I could bless others by
inviting them to enjoy my desires and then witnessing their joy. I
didn't need to partake physically to be fed spiritually. The Bread of
Life satisfied my deepest spiritual desires in a way no earthly bread

ever could. For as He promised, "I am the bread of life. Whoever comes to me will never be hungry, and whoever believes in me will never be thirsty" (John 6:35).

As I watched my family enjoy the things I couldn't, it struck me that my delight, born from sacrificial love, was exactly how Christ loves us from the cross. He gives from the depths of His sacrifice to bring about *His* greatest desire for *our* greatest joy—the possibility of being with Him forever. When we feed on Christ—through the sacraments and meditation on His Word—we are fueled by His supernatural life and love.

If you feel burdened by suffering, pain, or unfulfilled desires, look to the Bread of Life and become a well-fed soul strengthened to feed others. Like Christ, we are invited to allow God to transform our suffering into joy and resurrection for others. Jesus can—and will—fulfill our every longing in the end.

READING: JOHN 6:35

- Is it a surprise that Jesus desired to sacrifice His life to give us the possibility of joy? Sacrifice and joy may seem like unlikely companions. When has a sacrifice led to greater joy in your life?
- If food has been a source of stress with disordered eating or dietary restrictions, take comfort in the nourishment Jesus provides with His own Body and Blood in the Eucharist. How does this truth affect your heart?

INCOMPATIBLE DREAMS

TRAPPED ON A PATH

I chuckled at the blurry picture. Dancing brown eyes lit up a younger version of my smiling face. I cradled an infant against my Army uniform, while two toddlers stood on either side. The picture captured my last day serving in the Army before staying at home with my kids full-time. While my elation had been real, I also recalled a mix of loss and defeat behind that relieved smile.

I had always wanted to be a mother. As a young girl living at West Point, I had also decided I wanted to be in the Army. I would happily play with dolls, then join my dad on ruck marches with cadets. Every dream seemed possible as I sat on my dad's shoulders, my little pink-striped backpack swaying as we waded through the swamps.

In time, I became a cadet myself, married another cadet, and joined the real Army, hoping to eventually return to West Point to teach cadets. When our openness to God's timing brought children sooner than anticipated, I also became a doting mother. Yet my military supervisors publicly mocked our growing family, and many days after work, I had barely an hour with my kids before bedtime.

When my five-year Army contract ended, the dreams God planted in my heart felt like a total contradiction. For one dream to flourish, another had to die. I desperately wanted to be a great mom and a great leader, not an epic failure at both.

Yet God was waiting to forge a path from my apparent dead end.

Two short years after the photo was taken, I found myself back in the US Army Reserve with a one-weekend-a-month commitment, meaning I could still care for my kids at home full-time. Opportunities for writing, speaking, and ministry work flowed in—smaller dreams that I'd longed to invest in while on active duty but never had much time for. Before I knew it, I had even landed a local assignment teaching ROTC cadets on a schedule that fit perfectly with my family's schedule.

My "incompatible" dreams had come true after all—converging, by God's masterful hand, to form an infinitely richer reality. Like the dying grain of wheat that yielded an even greater harvest (see John 12:24), the grudging sacrifice of my one-dimensional dreams brought forth a three-dimensional life I could never have scripted. My seemingly closed doors opened to God's greater path, molding and refining me into the mother and leader He had created me to be all along.

Sometimes we chase goals and dreams relentlessly, yet find ourselves disillusioned when our expectations clash with reality. Other times we're overwhelmed with disappointment or grief when a closed door sounds like a resounding *no*. It can be tempting to believe the lies that God doesn't care or that He doesn't want good things for us.

Yet, in truth, God never plants dreams and desires just to snatch them away. He wants the very best for us—not just temporarily, but eternally. If you're facing a *no*, it could be an invitation to let God refine your desires into even greater realities. If you're grieving the death of a dream, consider whether the Lord is, in fact, cultivating a more abundant life and lasting grace for you.

Releasing our own narrow vision of life's dreams and desires frees God to do marvelous things—in His own time and in His eternally fruitful way. Even our lack of understanding can't prevent God from bringing life out of death. Let us keep dreaming and surrendering our dreams to Him, that He may produce ever more astonishing fruit in our lives.

READING: JOHN 12:24

- What dreams is God growing in your heart that you're too afraid to name? Whisper them to yourself now.
- Walk yourself through the death of a dream you've mourned. Now walk through it with Jesus holding you. How does this change your posture toward God and/ or your dream? Do you feel less alone?

LET'S KEEP DREAMING
AND SURRENDERING
OUR DREAMS TO HIM.

MEGAN HJELMSTAD

WEEK 16

NEW LIFE

FAITH ON THE PATH

"I'm afraid there's endometriosis everywhere." The surgeon spoke matter-of-factly, though not unkindly, as he pointed to one image after another. "The entire womb is extremely diseased. In addition to excision, I must recommend a total hysterectomy." I drew in a sharp breath and thanked him mechanically as I slid from the exam table, trying to process his words.

No more babies.

I held it together until I got to the car, then promptly crumpled against the steering wheel, chest heaving and tears streaming.

We had always dreamed of having a big family. During summer military training, I had slipped my then fiancé notes with sketches of us grinning and surrounded by a gaggle of kids in various stages of mischief. Once married, we'd remained open to life, committed wholeheartedly to practicing Natural Family Planning. Despite previous plans to delay children for a time due to our intense Army schedule, we welcomed two kids in quick succession.

Even with constant snide remarks and outright hostility from my military unit, we clung to the Church's beautiful, important teaching on openness to life—we could not deny Her truth that life was a gift, even when it was difficult or the timing didn't fit our perception of "perfect."

As the hostility increased around me, so did the pelvic pain I'd experienced since high school. When I sought out specialists, one warned, "If you want more kids, don't wait." God's timing became clear: had we waited according to our "plan" and left no room for God, we might have been left childless.

Within a year, I suffered an early miscarriage followed by an ectopic pregnancy where I was rushed into emergency surgery. That doctor's warning had become all too real. "Please," I whispered to my heavenly friend Saint Jude, patron of impossible causes. "Pray for just one more baby?" Within a month, I discovered I was pregnant, and our miracle baby was due, then born, on Saint Jude's feast day.

Years later, after countless prayers for healing and several more surgeries, it was time to accept my cross in a new way. I couldn't deny the prognosis; my womb posed a danger to me. Yet who would I be if I couldn't carry new life? After years of struggling to be open to life, I now wondered how I could have any other identity. Still, God was clearly inviting me down a path of spiritual motherhood—to bear new life through my heart and soul.

Once again, the Lord's plan quickly began to outshine my own. I was invited to lead a women's mentorship course and was astounded by the ongoing fruit. I started a church group that quietly covered our pastor in prayer every day. Most profoundly, I embraced new gratitude for the children God had already gifted us, which freed me to mother and love them even more intentionally.

We might think our plans are just as good or even better than God's design. However, believing—in word or in action—that our will is better than God's drastically limits the possibilities for His goodness. We stunt our own growth. When life diverges from plans we think best, or when we can't fathom a solution to our current situation, God sees our struggles. He cares. And He takes what appears broken or lost and redeems it beyond our wildest imagination.

"Your will be done, on earth as it is in heaven" (Matthew 6:10). If we seek to surrender to God's will above our own, He will infuse even the most difficult earthly realities with a taste of heaven. Our plans, relationships, and desires are always safest and most fruitful in His loving hands.

READING: MATTHEW 6:10

- Has God surprised you after you took a leap of faith? What did that look like or feel like?
- Make note of an obstacle to plans you've made. Now reexamine it. Is it an obstacle, or God redirecting traffic?

PART THREE

YOUR RELATIONSHIP WITH WHERE YOU CAME FROM

NELL O'LEARY

Let us take this time to ask ourselves: *How do I define myself based on who and where I came from?*

Family of origin and those around us as we grow into our identity have a profound impact on how we define ourselves. In this section, we'll walk through ten stories from my life—in contrasting pairs—that look at my relationship with my family of origin. I'll share suffering and joy in family, sadness in differences and happiness in similarities, poor habits and good habits, entanglement and individuation, along with conflict and resolution. I encourage you to open your Bible and follow along. Take time with the questions and let them sit inside your heart.

DIFFUSING JUDGMENTS

SUFFERING WITH FAMILY

I traced my finger along the wood paneling on the walls of our at-home library, inspecting the dust nestling into my fingerprint. I wondered how much dust had collected around the whole room. My attention ran up the panels and rushed back down to my mom's face. She was calling my name again and asking if I understood what she was saying.

"Yes." I nodded. "You and Dad still love us, but you are separating." My seven-year-old brain had no idea what that meant. I was just repeating back to her what she had told me.

My nine-year-old sister wondered if we would still go places all together, like her favorite restaurant. My little brother yanked at my teddy bear. My two oldest sisters, who were twelve and fourteen, probably knew what my mom was crying about.

After a few hugs and other conversation about what would become my parents' impending divorce, the three youngest of us were ushered out of the room. We made our way into the kitchen, wrestled into our sneakers and ponchos for the biting autumn air, and then raced outside to our jungle gym. Between swings, I thought to myself, *I should have worn socks.*

As I grew up, people would ask me about my family, and I would couch my parents' divorce in the happiest terms possible. "They're divorced, but they always co-parented so well together!" I figured if I could diffuse any judgments about their divorce, then people wouldn't think less of me or our family.

You probably have that one thing you leap in front of to explain before someone asks too much about it. The dysfunction in your family, the choices of your loved ones. Or maybe your suffering hides in your heart vault, and no one could ferret it out of you. Truly, the anticipation of judgment can be harsher than the actual words themselves. We worry that our suffering will define us.

I certainly felt defined by my parents' divorce, especially in Catholic circles. Occasionally people would pry into *why* they had divorced. Mostly people behaved as if it were contagious, as if I were the product of brokenness and could break up their own families. I quickly came to know the sting of being lumped into the "sinful" category based on my parents' choices.

Maybe you have known suffering in your family because of circumstances outside of your control, whether that be surviving an assault, enduring chronic illness, or contending with a complex family shuffle. Our family-of-origin wounds don't necessarily break us, though, do they? Sometimes they give us softer hearts for others in pain. Certainly God's grace makes this possible. Through it all, God reminds us that even our suffering can give Him glory.

In the Gospel of John, there was a man born blind "so that God's works might be revealed in him" (John 9:3). Jesus healed this man who had known suffering all his life as surely as He desires to heal us from our suffering. It may be suffering we aren't even aware of anymore because we've numbed for survival—He wants to take that from us too.

And while we're in the thick of the mess, the reverberations of our broken hearts beat right within His Sacred Heart. He knew from the beginning of time how our stories would unfold. He knew the particulars of our pain, our suffering, and how we would try to deflect judgment about it and hide within it.

However you're feeling defined by the brokenness of your family of origin, invite God into this jumbled knot. He can show His love and glory in both my parents' divorce when I was so little and in your own pocket of pain. Can we let Him do this today?

READING: JOHN 9:1–3

- Do you struggle with being defined by your suffering? Do you feel judgment for the brokenness in your family? Take a deep breath and try to detach yourself from the struggle or suffering now.

- Someone in your life is silently struggling today. How can you be Jesus to that person in his or her suffering? Check your heart for softness and invite Jesus to deepen your sympathy and empathy.

OUR LORD KNEW
FROM THE BEGINNING
OF TIME HOW OUR
STORIES WOULD
UNFOLD.

NELL O'LEARY

CONVERSION AGAIN AND AGAIN

JOY IN FAMILY

"Peter!" I shouted up the stairs at 7:52 a.m. "I'm leaving *now*!" I slammed my backpack down on the second stair as if the reverberations would convince a fifteen-year-old boy that his ride to Sunday Mass, aka his older sister, was indeed leaving. I got into my hand-me-down car in the driveway, laid on the horn, and contemplated just driving off. If he was responsible enough to serve on the altar, surely he could be responsible enough to set his own alarm clock.

Peter slid down the stairs, popped a coat over one shoulder, switched off the kitchen lights, and barely shut the back door behind him. "You're so rude," he said as he got in the car, no sign of appreciation.

When our older sister had graduated, we not only lost the glue that kept the three youngest in our family together, we also lost our diplomatic intermediary, who ensured we were at school, church, and sports practices on time. My resentment over now being the responsible one spilled out often and loudly, while my brother remained aloof and detached from my demands for punctuality and respect.

But as we went our separate ways for college—me to a huge state school in our hometown with no Catholics in sight, and him to a small Catholic liberal arts school outside of DC—surprisingly, it was going to Mass together that closed the relationship gap. I was hanging on to our shared Catholic faith for dear life, flailing with bad habits, and he seemed to have blossomed into his faith life.

On my first visit to his college, *he* picked *me* up from Dulles International Airport, and *on time*. We drove out to Front Royal and walked the riverbanks, praying the Rosary with his friends, and then brunched, enjoying copious bacon on a family friend's sprawling lawn. We listened to the cicadas purr in the night air as we psychoanalyzed our family and watched clips of *Arrested Development*. We worshiped at Mass together.

Interestingly enough, when you start rooting your life in the same faith as a sibling or a friend or a person you're dating, you start to trust his or her judgment in other areas too. When my brother started encouraging me to examine my dating patterns, I actually listened because he was living out the truth of his own advice. We are sort of like sheep that way. We can step out of the shadow of doubt when we're tucked in behind someone else who is stepping out first.

As I watched him during college and graduate school, I saw that being Catholic wasn't a carefully selected garment he and his friends donned on Sunday mornings between 9 and 10:30 a.m. It was a continuous way of life. And it was so appealing. Who knew that my haphazard teenage brother would turn into an intentional lover of the Lord and be the one to influence *me*?

The Lord Jesus didn't come find me on a cliff as the shepherd did to find his lost sheep in this week's scripture. He sent my own little brother to call me back, to show me not only the way back, but the way to be fully alive as a Catholic adult. I'm pretty sure Jesus was whispering down to Peter, "Rejoice with me, for I have found my sheep that was lost" (Luke 15:6).

Some of us have one big life conversion, but most of us have little conversions along the way, bringing us back into the fold or connecting us deeper to God. Our little conversions can happen by simply observing how someone else lives or acknowledging we may be more lost than we look. And it may just be a family member who leads us back into the family of God.

The Lord rejoices over your heart turning toward Him, for the first time or the hundredth time. And His joy echoes into our family relationships and actually feeds them with joy too. My brother's faith inspired my own, and we were both more joyful as a result. Let us continue to turn our hearts back to Christ and rejoice alongside Him.

READING: LUKE 15:6–7

- If you're lost, sister, whom will you look to for help in getting back to the Lord? If you're on firm ground, whom will you rejoice over after your example, encouragement, or prayer brings them the peace that only Jesus can provide?
- Maybe today is the day you reach out in confidence to a wavering or unsure little sheep in your life. To whom would you like to reach out today?

SPLITTING THE ROAD

SADNESS IN DIFFERENCES

We sat at a round restaurant table with a menu full of Dutch delights. My brother passed me the butter for the rolls heaped in front of me, my sister poured some room-temperature mineral water, and my sister's boyfriend smoothed his hand over his hair as he remarked, "It just seems like there could be a god or not, but our belief or disbelief doesn't really change that."

The humid end-of-summer air in Amsterdam swept through the open window behind him as I cleared my throat, gave a look to my brother, and finished buttering a sesame roll. We were all here for a close family friend's wedding, brought together for peace and harmony.

I hoped my brother could convince our future brother-in-law that Catholicism was the religion most compatible with the psychology of the human person. I scraped the dregs of the butter out of the little ramekin and prayed to my sister's guardian angel to intercede and help her come back around to the faith.

My heart sank back into its tired yet hopeful posture. She wasn't going to be convinced this time. I swallowed hard and hid a tear in my napkin as I thanked the waiter in advance for more sesame rolls.

I suppose the crying had first begun when my sister moved away after she graduated college, where we had lived together with her miniature American Eskimo dog, who barked incessantly. All through college, I would bring her my misunderstandings with friends and drama with crushes, and she would help me make sense of it all.

After her move, she slowly drifted away from practicing our shared Catholic faith. I felt left behind and somehow rejected, as though she was leaving me along with the Church and its teachings. It was then that I learned to take things to God first, to ground my identity in Him and not in a person, not even my best friend and sister. I would also have to start trusting more—trusting that my sister and I could still be close even as we disagreed on things like the afterlife, sin, or miracles.

So when we dined in Amsterdam years later, me having just finished my federal clerkship after law school and her being years deep into a design profession in New York City, I still held out hope she would return to the faith, and in doing so, maybe more deeply accept me.

Have you split the road in two with someone you loved and watched him or her leave what you shared behind? It is heart-wearyingly hard. And you might have to truly mourn the change or loss. But the mourning isn't the end. It cracks open our hearts to God, the Source of all love and comfort. Jesus tells us Himself, "Blessed are those who mourn, for they will be comforted" (Matthew 5:4). He doesn't tell us that our reason for mourning will be obviated. He simply says that we will receive comfort.

Loving people when we disagree is a deeper invitation to grow through our discomfort. We may feel disconnected or rejected in the chasm of our differences, but Our Lord allows us to experience those feelings to deepen our trust in Him and His ultimate plan. In those moments, we must give up our semblance of control.

Let your loved one, your child, your spouse, your beloved friend move along his or her path, even if it's not the path you want. Love that person, and pray for his or her footfalls all along the way. And if it hurts? We can trust God with our tears.

READING: MATTHEW 5:4

- Has someone close to you changed his or her beliefs or grown apart from you on a shared path? How can you best love that individual where he or she is right now?

- Are you mourning a change in your life? A job, a relationship, a disappointment in yourself? Bring this to the Lord. He longs to comfort you.

SUFFERING CRACKS
OPEN OUR HEARTS TO GOD,
THE SOURCE OF ALL
LOVE AND COMFORT.

NELL O'LEARY

INVITATIONS TO LOVE

HAPPINESS IN SIMILARITIES

I squeezed my hair dry, listened to my newborn's chirpy cries downstairs, and quickly ran a brush through the snarls in my hair. I practiced the diaphragmatic breathing I was supposed to do daily to help my C-section recovery. I peered down at my cracked toenails and made a mental note to ask my husband to trim them.

The cries died down and were replaced with the sounds of my sister and her husband cooing at our three-week-old boy, baby number five. Instead of the painful trek back down to join them, I braced my palms against my abdomen and sat down. No position was without its jabs and jolts of pain, but this way they could enjoy him, and I the break.

They were still newlyweds, having found each other later in life, and they shared a love of my kids. The baby squeaked as they took turns tucking his arm into the blanket, fussing over his neck position, and (I imagined) smiling at each other.

Moments later, the four older children rushed through the door, crowding in on the baby, claiming a toe to squeeze, a cheek to kiss. My own siblings and I grew up as an Irish-Catholic clan of five kids, and like my children, we were on top of each other all the time. Even now, our spouses exchange knowing glances as we talk over each other with inside jokes.

It's a privilege to share history with family members, or friends who are like family. But family also comes with its own challenges, spoken and unspoken. It's tempting to pick through your clan's faults. It's easy to keep family members in the same boxes since childhood—she's the negative one, she's the inconsiderate one, and so on. This sister and I weren't always close, but I'm poised to witness the happy intersection of our families in the here and now.

My loud, brimming house with now five kids overflows into my sister and her husband's yard down the block. Our stories are still being written together, through the next generation, which is joyful and healing. My sister and my brother-in-law bless our five with their interest in origami, math puzzles, and an example of living out our shared faith. I keep inviting them, pushing past whatever annoyances arise in sibling relationships, grateful they even want to come into our mess.

An ongoing relationship requires continual invitation. This week's scripture is the parable of the wedding feast, where the invited guests decided not to come. The master of the house then widened the invitation: "Go out into the roads and lanes, and compel people to come in, so that my house may be filled" (Luke 14:23). God will find a way to invite everyone in. He so desires His house to be filled!

My own small act of invitation that day for my sister and brother-in-law to experience the baby has nothing on the glorious invite to the banquet in heaven. And yet, when we examine our relationships within the context of our families, we need to check our invitation lists. Do we just include our easy-to-handle family members for picture-perfect events? Do we continue to invite in love those family members who are harder to deal with? Is everyone invited into our authentic lives, where our needs are shown, where we are vulnerable to judgment? It's tempting to cull people, to confine our lists to the convenient and favorite.

Look past the obvious invitees to those who want to share in your joy. It doesn't cost much, but the return of sharing happiness and inviting others into love is priceless.

READING: LUKE 14:23

- Whom can you invite closer into your story? If something is holding you back, talk it over with a close confidante, and then pray about it.
- If your invitations have been ignored and that pain still wounds you, what is Jesus inviting you to understand about yourself or the person you invited? Be humble and receive the lesson.

UNHELPFUL HELPINGS

POOR HABITS

I turned to my husband to complain, "My brother just forgot to tell the rest of *his* sisters when he's coming, and some people work, and it's a whole debacle because people need to request days off or at least reschedule meetings. . . ." He smiled and turned back to his newspaper. "Sounds like it doesn't involve you," he noted quietly before turning over to the back page.

I sent the text anyway: "When are you arriving with your dog, wife, kids?"

Our brother hadn't named his arrival date, probably because he didn't know it yet. His family of three little kiddos, one large dog, and one pregnant wife were driving across the country to come visit us before they moved abroad. Despite these facts, I couldn't help but try to help. My version of helping, that is, which is talking to every sibling about the unknowns of the trip's schedule, assuaging scheduling snafus for some, planning grocery shopping lists for others.

"Maybe I should round back to my sister," I started to say before my husband's half-incredulous, half-laughing expression stopped me. "Never mind. I'll let them figure it out."

A lesson I have had to learn over and over in life is to get out of the way. It's extremely tempting to offer "just one more" round of advice, "just one last" hint of help, or "just a quick" correction or redirection on any—and I mean practically *any*—set of circumstances. Even this benign, jam-packed visit by family from out of town belied my poor habit of being "helpful," which often means I'm just too involved.

You may also be tempted to offer your gifts of organization, communication, or problem-solving—gifts that, when unpaid for and unsolicited, are not valued or wanted. At the heart of my fervently offered help is always the same thing: I long to be valued as priceless, indispensable, appreciated beyond measure for what I have done. News flash: it doesn't work like that. When I give my unasked-for "help," no one remarks on how thoughtful it was and praises my caring heart. They are equal parts oblivious or annoyed, and I'm left feeling frustrated and devalued.

Equally noteworthy is that when we step in to try to solve issues between others, we rob them of the opportunity to deal with them themselves, for their relationships to widen and deepen. Resolving other people's problems is a temporary maneuver because without the chance for them to work them out, you just have to keep stepping in again and again.

Matthew 7:3 reminds us that Jesus asked, "Why do you see the speck in your neighbor's eye, but do not notice the log in your own eye?" Instead of worrying about what was happening between my siblings, I could have taken the opportunity to evaluate my own many shortcomings in communication. This habit of inserting myself to feel helpful, valued, important, whatever you want to call it, needed to stop.

Where do you find yourself missing your weaknesses, your poor habits, the logs in your eye? What needs examination today, sister? A habit can be remade, and often that happens when we replace it with another one. However you find yourself regularly identifying your friends' and family members' struggles, stop yourself from commenting. Hold back on the advice or commentary. Replace those thoughts with a prayer of love and gratitude for their lives. God knows they have endured the many logs in your eye. Take any struggle with hypocrisy to prayer today.

Remember: there is freedom in knowing our inestimable value in God's eyes. The gift of the sacrament of confession will help remind you of how you're loved. Try to make it there this week.

READING: MATTHEW 7:3–5

- Do you find yourself tempted to comment, help, advise when not asked? What is at the root of that?
- Does this sound like you in your family or in your relationships? How has it affected your relationships? If you are the more phlegmatic, go-with-the-flow one, how have you handled the poor habits of others?

THERE IS FREEDOM
IN KNOWING OUR
INESTIMABLE VALUE
IN GOD'S EYES.

NELL O'LEARY

SERVING UNSEEN

GOOD HABITS

"Add the Italian seasoning packet," my mom said as she emphasized the *I* in *Italian*. "Then the roast can just sit in the slow cooker for hours." How hard could it be? Steam some baby carrots and call me a chef.

"Your father can drive it over there if you need him to. Do you have those disposable serving tins?"

I smiled. "That's okay, Mom. I want to meet them myself."

A chance connection from a law school friend had connected me to a family whose baby had major health issues. They were staying at the Ronald McDonald house. This provided me with an opportunity to make a meal. I looked in the fridge briefly, seeing nothing for our own dinner, let alone what I needed for this meal. "Mom, could you ask Dad if he wouldn't mind running into the grocery store on his way? I don't actually have any of the ingredients."

My pregnancy with our second had laid me low, and homemade-meal nights were few and far between. But at twenty-four weeks along, it was time I got back into preparing dinners other than graham crackers and milk, Honeycrisp apples, and slices of cheddar. And with my own toddler, I could only imagine what this family was going through. I wanted to meet this suffering mother, be able to press some food into her hands, and make sure she knew we wanted to help.

The shredded beef dinner was my mom's go-to for anyone in need. I'd seen her sprinkle that packet of seasoning for deaths and births, divorces and surgeries, moves and college send-offs. She'd be wrapping tinfoil over the top faster than you could ask if she'd made chocolate chip cookies to go with (always).

But in between defrosting a chuck roast and tinfoiling it, I never heard her ask anyone if they wanted the food. I would just catch the tail end of a conversation: "I'll drop something by right before dinner, so warm your oven." She figured that if she would have tentatively offered help at a future date, no one would say yes.

Women have been bringing other women meals to ease their burdens since the first Neanderthal woman figured those wild berries complemented that wild arugula. This habit of helping, of meeting unrequested needs, is hidden but powerful. When we see someone in need and allow her to experience feeling seen, we are giving much more than just a meal or a gift—we are acknowledging her and her pain. "Yes, you matter," these meals tell her. "Yes, you are seen," we say as we rip open Italian seasoning over a cow carcass on our countertop.

Jesus reminded us in this week's scripture to not make a big, outward show of our spiritual actions or piety. You shouldn't worry about being seen by others, "but by your Father who is in secret;

and your Father who sees in secret will reward you" (Matthew 6:18). Instead of the affirmation, applause, and appreciation of others, the Father's reward should be our motivating factor. God desires us to grow in good habits, to serve Him and others in a hidden way, a way that is not about us at all.

Can you do something good for someone else and receive no credit? Does the thought leave you chafing a little? As someone who craves affirmation, it does for me. But when I think about doing little acts of love, offering up my inconveniences for a friend in need, dropping off a meal or even just dessert, sending money to a stranger's cause, I want to do those things for God's honor and glory and as a big thank-You to Him.

He's given us so much, sister. Let us make a habit of giving back to others, one slow cooker at a time.

READING: MATTHEW 6:18

- Are you presented with opportunities to serve unseen, to meet a need without being asked? Pay attention quietly.
- Examine your life and find where you are able to give extra. Is it a financial donation to a worthy cause? Is it committing to volunteer regularly? Is it providing a meal when you see the need? Think about this.

CHRISTMAS WAFFLE TRADITION

ENTANGLEMENT

As my friend leaned in, her voice dropped considerably. "So then we spent Christmas morning at my parents' house, unwrapping *their* gifts for the kids after a long Christmas Eve at my in-laws'. The Christmas dinner was actually like a late lunch, and of course, my kids wouldn't eat anything except pies by that point, and my brother and his wife were horrified because their son is six months old and they can't imagine a child ever having temper tantrums over turkey drumsticks being 'sticky.' Don't even ask about Mass at my in-laws' church." She groaned deeply and rolled her eyes.

I swirled my oversized cup of hot cocoa, catching the last vestiges of the whipping cream. It was our regular January catch-up at our local coffee shop, and almost every year I heard a variation of these dynamics. "So when you told your mother-in-law that you guys were going to do Christmas Day just with your kids and husband, she said to go for it?"

"Not in this lifetime." She pushed her chair back to get a wet napkin for her toddler's hands, which were covered with a caramel roll. I thought about my family's new tradition of Christmas morning waffles, just our little family of four, and uttered a prayer of gratitude under my breath.

The truth was we lived with my parents and one of my sisters in a big, old house, so it actually *was* a big deal to have our Christmas morning with just us. After agonizing over how the idea would be received, I finally broached the topic that maybe my husband and our two little kiddos should have some time during the holiday when we opened our presents for each other and celebrated Baby Jesus' birthday with waffles before church. Our housemates weren't offended, and a new tradition was born.

But the other truth was that I had agonized over the conversation as a newish mom in her late twenties because I didn't want to upset the family I had come from by choosing the family I was growing. I had worried more about that potentially tense dynamic than if our little family would grow with our own memories.

It turns out you can set a healthy boundary when those involved are motivated by the joy and love of being together. By prioritizing Christmas-morning waffles with my little unit, I was setting a boundary, while honoring the rest of the day with the larger group. And this boundary didn't mean I didn't love the rest of my family. Boundaries and love are not mutually exclusive.

However, I know family and relationships with loved ones can be complicated. My girlfriend felt trapped in a situation that may be familiar to you. It could be family expectations at the holidays, friends' expectations at happy hour, or annual birthday traditions.

Your need to meet someone else's desires outpaces your ability to admit that the expectation isn't working for you anymore. That crippling anxiety is what Our Lord wants to free us of based on this week's scripture for reflection.

"And can any of you by worrying add a single hour to your span of life?" (Luke 12:25). Answer: *no*. It's a wasted effort. Worrying about how my family will react to my choices has taken up enormous emotional real estate in my mind throughout the years. And, no, it has not changed their reactions! I have tasted the freedom of letting go of my desired outcome. When I've made choices based on my little family's needs, and not based on worry, I've found greater peace. I want that for you too, sister.

Today might be the day you shed your worries about what would happen if you adjusted a boundary with your family. Ask the Holy Spirit in prayer for guidance, take heart, and set your worry aside.

READING: LUKE 12:25–26

- Can you easily identify a boundary that you'd like to set with your family but haven't? Be gentle with yourself but honest about what's going on there.
- If a worry or an anxious thought about family boundaries keeps coming up, talk it over with a trusted friend, spiritual director, or counselor. What is the first step to shedding it?

ASK THE HOLY
SPIRIT IN PRAYER
FOR GUIDANCE
AND TAKE HEART.

NELL O'LEARY,

TAKING A WILD LEAP

INDIVIDUATION

As we crossed from Minnesota into Wisconsin, I began a slow drip of tears. Traveling at seventy-five miles per hour, my dad glanced down at his printed-out directions and told me to prepare the coins for the tolls ahead as we headed toward Michigan.

"What time will we stop again?" I aimed my face toward the window to delay the discovery of my tears. I just didn't want to hear it again: my mom's assurances that I would make friends, while I insisted that I should never have left my horses to go to law school.

"We have a full tank, sweetie. It will be a while," my dad said and then followed up, "but you wouldn't have liked staying in town for law school anyway. What do they call the person who graduated last in her class? Lawyer!"

My mom and I chuckled. It worked; my dad had lifted the mood. But both schools I had been admitted to were Catholic, so why did I have to go to the one a dozen hours away by car? I guess individuating from my family had been part of the draw. But now that we were halfway there, I had my doubts.

In the quiet pocket of my heart, the Lord had called me to this wild leap to move across states. My whole life I had followed in the footsteps of my older sisters with school, ballet lessons, and choir camp. They always impressed the adults in their lives, so I was stepping into a very well-cast set of shadows. I had a comfortable life in the Twin Cities: horses I trained and showed, restaurants I frequented, and ride-or-die family members whom I could complain to or mooch a grilled cheese sandwich off of.

Maybe the reasons to stay were the same as those to go.

I had an easy life with a supportive family—someone to drop off a meal, a house to stay in, or a caring person to help sort my problems. But this move meant I would need to build new relationships not predicated on whom someone in my family knew. I would be my own safety net.

We are presented with opportunities for growth when we leave our safety zones, our known quantities, our self-limiting predictions. Yes, we may flounder (like my Federal Taxation grade), but lessons learned through failure are of inestimable worth. And our victories are our own, and so much sweeter.

You don't have to move far away to experience growth opportunities; you can find them in your own backyard. Jesus said that "no one who has left house or brothers or sisters or mother or father or children or fields, for my sake . . . will not receive a hundredfold now in this age . . . and in the age to come eternal life" (Mark 10:29–30). When you leave the comforts of home and family in the pursuit of God's will, He will use that for your good and His glory.

Leaving family and fields looks different for different people. In my case, I needed to move away to prove to myself that I could do things on my own. I also needed the quiet to hear and discern God's will in my life.

Your discernment might happen in the loud chaos of your busy family, sister. Your individuation might look less like driving across state lines and more like setting a necessary boundary with a family member over a holiday dinner. God blesses us when we leave that which we are called away from and when we draw closer to Him in the process.

We're made for God, to be reunited with Him for all eternity. He encourages us to trust Him, even in those steps we take away from our families to follow His call. He is with us every mile of the way.

READING: MARK 10:29–30

- Is there a discernment on the horizon for you that might take you out of your comfort zone emotionally or physically? Bring it specifically to Our Lord in prayer.
- Have you had to build or rebuild your own safety net? What has that been like? Take heart that God has walked with you and always will, even when you don't sense Him.

FALSE CONTROL AND GREEN BEANS

EXTENDED FAMILY CONFLICT

Many, many years after my tearful drive to law school, I found myself in a different car, tears welling up for an entirely different reason. I stared out my minivan's passenger window as we whipped past house after house, straw hat itching my forehead, nearly to church for Easter Sunday Mass. My lashes held these tears, spilling some, blinking back others. *I'm worried about you*, my husband's words echoed in my head. I pressed my fingers against my temples as my three-month-old baby fussed in the back seat and the four older children squabbled with general disquietude.

My fingers still smelled like the garlic I had diced earlier for our roasted potato dish. My wrists were sore from rolling out dough for pie crusts. My fingernails sported green corners from the bean tips I had snapped off for a green bean casserole with lemon rinds.

Maybe I'm stressed because I spent all morning cooking for Easter brunch for my extended family, and maybe I'm tired because I spent all day yesterday cleaning the house, and maybe I was also nursing a little baby every five minutes?

I couldn't answer his worried observation. It crushed me. I thought I looked as though I had everything under control. My stomach incision throbbed, my hormones were all over the place, and the baby hadn't slept more than two hours straight since he was born. Clearly this all was not under control.

I was so driven to cook an Easter meal at my house to regain control over my life after another hyperemesis pregnancy, my fifth one, only worse because it had taken place during a pandemic with distance learning for two of my kids. I wanted to definitively demonstrate that I was healed after my first C-section birth, which wasn't even true! I should have let go of controlling everything and broadcasting that I was *fine*, and instead taken care of my physical and mental health.

The truth is that depending on extended family for help, or maybe friends who are like family in your case, presents a yo-yo feeling. *Yes, I want and need the help. No, I don't want to ask for help or look needy.* Asking for help opens us up to the possibility of criticism. We can feel over a barrel, beholden, suddenly vulnerable in the worst way.

I quietly, desperately, wanted to get "back" to whatever normal was left in my life. And being in control of our side dishes at Easter brunch, or how our lives look when examined up close and personal by the people helping us, gives us a false sense of control over our actual existence.

Jesus reminds us through His words to the disciples in this week's scripture that we are not in control. He said, "I can do nothing on my own" (John 5:30). Everything He did while walking this earth was dependent on God the Father's will for Him. Sister, if Jesus, who is God, did nothing on His own, who are we to pretend we do anything on our own? Our very existence is willed by God.

You may be self-reliant and independent. Or you may feel incapable of doing much of anything. However you function, the interior truth is the same: without God, we can do nothing. And we know He uses subsidiaries, messengers, those amazing people on earth we call friends and family, to help us. They can help us when we're down, and they can help us discern His will.

God's will for me was to humbly accept my family's help and to stop trying to prove I didn't need help. Contemplate His will for you and how you can let go of control and be authentic in your need for Him.

READING: JOHN 5:30

- Do you struggle with wanting to be in control and to appear to have it all together? Think about a time you realized you weren't and you didn't. Find the lesson and rest in God's tenderness there.
- Who is someone in your family or friend circle who has been there for you during a particularly hard time? Remember to thank that treasured individual. If you're that person to someone else, appreciate the grace God gave you to help.

CONTEMPLATE
THE LORD'S WILL
FOR YOU.

NELL O'LEARY

FACE THE BAGGAGE

EXTENDED FAMILY RESOLUTION

My mom's voice caught as I leaned in for a hug while she continued to speak: "I just didn't expect you to lay into me like that, and I am sorry too." She sniffled and wiped generally at her face. I scooted closer to her in the little French restaurant, bouncing the baby on my lap while tucking an arm behind her.

"I know, Mom. I know," I said. "You didn't deserve to have me pile on you during an already tender time." Her sister was in the ICU, and she had just returned from a trip to the West Coast to be at her sister's bedside with her other siblings. It probably wasn't the right time to unfurl a list of complaints from my childhood.

We finished our crème brûlée. The baby fussed excessively. I lingered at the table for a moment after scribbling my name on the charge slip. This was one of the first times I had apologized to my mom for critiquing her parenting without backpedaling on the fact that there were underlying issues to be addressed. I murmured to the baby, fumbled in my oversized purse to tuck my credit card away, and met my mom at the exit to walk home.

For many years, I confused peacemaking with covering over any conflict, people pleasing, and burying my emotional response to my life. Peace looked like external tranquility, like everyone coexisting perfectly. Peace looked like not questioning our family's narrative on . . . well, anything.

In reality, I was simply mistaken. Every single family, mine included, has problems. And being a mom myself now means that I examine my childhood and adolescence and question why my parents made *those* choices and why they responded *that* way. Now I am presented with my own mothering choices and opportunities to respond to. I have to face my past to know how to deal with my present.

You have your own family stuff, the emotional suitcases you've misplaced, buried, or burned. And in the name of peace, you might not want to find it, sort through it, acknowledge it. But peace and peacemaking come from the pursuit of deep honesty.

That evening over crème brûlée, my mistake was being insensitive to my mom. My mistake was not wanting to charitably and gently uncover family habits and parts of our story that bothered me. Actually doing so might bring about an opportunity for real peace for both of us.

Jesus, the Prince of Peace Himself, in this week's scripture for reflection told us, "Blessed are the peacemakers, for they will be called children of God" (Matthew 5:9). Jesus modeled this for us by relentlessly bringing peace, both by drawing people to His Sacred Heart, the furnace of peace, and by reminding them to make peace with their neighbors, family, and frenemies before coming into God's presence (see Matthew 5:24).

In our families and in our stories, God invites us to be peace-makers and to bring His peace. We cannot bring what we don't have, so as His children, we pray and plead for our own peace. Peace with any trauma, any wounds, and disappointments in our families. Peace with situations we can never rectify, memories we can only forgive and release. Peace with mistakes made and words spoken that can never be unheard.

Peace doesn't mean blindfolded backpedaling. In my instance, it means speaking the wound and forgiving my imperfect but loving parents, who did their best. Peacemaking means asking God to guide your pursuit of peace, sister. He holds it; He shares it; He wants it for your heart so much. Allow His healing rays of peace into your story now.

READING: MATTHEW 5:9

- What unspoken habits do you find yourself falling into to make peace at any cost in your family?
- If you're afraid to speak about an underlying family issue because it will rock the boat, reconsider it in light of Jesus being the Source of true peace. Is He calling you to bring it out today?

PART FOUR

YOUR
RELATIONSHIP
WITH LOVE
AND FAMILY

BONNIE ENGSTROM

Let us take this time to ask ourselves: *How do I grow in my capacity to love despite and through the challenges of love and family life?*

In the previous section, we looked at relationships with the family who raised us and formed us. In this section, we'll look at the family we make and choose. We'll walk through ten stories from my life—in contrasting pairs. I'll share young and unconditional love, focusing on self and then on others, neglecting and learning self-care, communicating from past wounds and a place of love, and feeling disconnected as a family and then connecting together. I encourage you to open your Bible and follow along. Take time with the questions and let them sit inside your heart.

RIVALS AND ROSARIES

INEXPERIENCED LOVE

My finger and thumb moved to the next bead. Imagining the Joyful Mystery of the Nativity, I prayed for her some day to have easy labors. The next bead, blessings in her future marriage and motherhood. Every day for a week, I prayed the Joyful Mysteries for this woman, asking that the best in life would pass me so she could enjoy many blessings instead.

It may sound holy, but it was false piety. I had no devotion to the Blessed Mother and no great love for the woman for whom I prayed. She was my boyfriend's ex-girlfriend. Though she still had feelings for him, he insisted on continuing a friendship with her, and that meant, in my mind, that she was my rival. As I prayed these prayers, I experienced no growing peace. The only thing that flowed was tears; the only thing that deepened was sadness.

My prayers of humility were full of false humility because they were rooted in a twisted belief that God would be pleased to withhold all goodness from me. With every bead, my prayers really were statements about what I thought of myself: unattractive, unintelligent, and unlovable. While praying half-heartedly for this other woman, I was really just thinking of myself. Hopefully the Lord still blessed her, and hopefully Mary and Jesus interceded for me too.

I was too young to understand real love. I had read many British novels and knew that love stories usually ended happily, with large houses and large sums of money. Also, love was supposed to be complicated, even torturous. It seemed that married life was just as often about grinning and bearing it as about two people who truly loved and respected each other. My boyfriend was trying to be kind by maintaining the friendship with his ex, so for his sake, I thought I needed to grin and bear tense conversations, group events, and pitiful Rosaries.

The truth was I didn't have a clue what love really was. I had only experienced dating relationships that were based on the spark of chemistry; it would be years before I knew the joy of a romantic love rooted in abiding friendship. I didn't know that it didn't need to be so hard; I didn't realize there was enough of God's grace and goodness for both of us, my rival and me.

Maybe you have been immature or inexperienced in love too. Maybe you know what it's like to think you deserve the leftovers, to believe that you're never enough. Maybe you know what it's like to accept this idea that you are unlovable.

But sister, that's not the truth.

In the scripture we are pondering this week, Jesus insisted that we should love our enemies (Luke 6:35). I thought my enemy was this other woman, but it was me. Before I could experience any healthy relationships, I had to let God love me. I had to love myself. We are invited to surrender our self-hatred to God so we can live in the freedom of loving and being generous toward ourselves and our rivals.

God the Father loves us as His own precious children. We have not earned that relationship, but Jesus Christ—God the Son—has claimed us and brought us into it. We love rightly when we belong to Jesus, and through Him we love as the Father loves. In this, we are truly children of the Most High. And there is no leftover love in God's family.

READING: LUKE 6:35

- Can you think back on a time when you felt immature in your idea of what love was or how it should look? Invite God into that memory and ask His light to draw you deeper.
- Does the idea of letting God love you bring you joy or trepidation? Start praying for this today.

WE ARE TRULY
CHILDREN OF THE
MOST HIGH.

BONNIE ENGSTROM

SAFE AND SECURE

UNCONDITIONAL LOVE

The crack of lightning and the clap of thunder were close, almost on top of each other. I awoke to the dark house brightening for a moment and felt it shake from the deep, rolling rumbles of the thunderstorm. That's when my fifteen-month-old cried out.

I dashed across the hall to his bedroom, where the rain slammed against old windowpanes, and I climbed into his toddler bed, scooping him into my arms and pulling him close to my chest. With his head tucked under my chin, I tried to calm him, and even though his tears stopped, he would not settle.

Trying to distract him, I asked if he wanted a drink or maybe a warmer blanket. No response. Finally, exhausted and out of ideas, I asked if he wanted his dad. He nodded, and I carried him to our room. As he laid his head on my husband's arm, I whispered to my husband the sequence of the night's events. By the time I had circled the bed and lain down alongside them, both father and son were tucked in and fast asleep. Though the storm continued to rage, that little boy stayed asleep the rest of the night.

I could have been annoyed that all my work to pacify my child was not sufficient, but instead I was so grateful. Between my husband and me, we were able to give our children a sense of security, not because we were perfect parents, but because we both knew the unconditional love of God the Father. In particular, my husband modeled this for me and our family every day.

At that moment in the middle of that stormy night, my heart swelled.

With my toddler nestled into the safety of his father's arms, completely secure, I was also able to lie down feeling completely secure. My sweet little boy respected the gentle strength and humble confidence of his daddy, and in the arms of his father, my son knew that he was safe. We could all rest because we were filled with trust.

No marriage, no family, no relationship is perfect. Storms and hard seasons come, and we can't always calm them. But with the Lord's grace, you and I can repeatedly surrender and entrust our loved ones to God. He transforms us, making it possible for us to accept and share His unconditional love.

This week's scripture from Saint Luke's Gospel reminds us of Jesus' calming of the storm for the disciples, "They went to him and woke him up, shouting, 'Master, Master, we are perishing!' And he woke up and rebuked the wind and the raging waves; they ceased, and there was a calm" (Luke 8:24). Everyone in the boat was afraid and needed comfort, just as my son was scared of the storm and needed his father's care. By rebuking the wind and the waves for the doubting disciples, Jesus showed that God provides for us unconditionally, no matter our sins, our wounds, or our fears.

We can trust in God's gentle strength, rely on His humble confidence, and find comfort in His arms. You may feel that you have been left to weather the storm alone and afraid, but I invite you to let the Blessed Mother carry you to her Son. Let Him place you in the Father's righteous right hand that you may be comforted and protected.

READING: LUKE 8:22–25

- God's comfort is for all of us. Is there a portion of your woundedness you're holding back from Him because you don't believe that? Take it to Him now.
- Walk through a memory of a time you felt alone, frightened, or abandoned. Did anyone in particular comfort you? Give thanks for that comforter in prayer.

LOVE LIKE GOD

SELF-FOCUSED

The glass bowl teetered on top of a pot of boiling water as my daughter stirred a stick of butter and high-quality baking chocolate together. The sifted flour and other dry ingredients sat in a larger bowl on the dusty counter. Next to that was a third one, filled with sugar and farm-fresh eggs. The hand mixer's beaters perched over half the bowl, dripping some golden, eggy sugar onto the counter.

I reached into that mysterious place where moms find patience and took a deep breath. My preteen was in her element, and she beamed when I entered the kitchen. "Mom! I'm making a cake! Dad said I could!"

I forced a smile and agreed as I read over her recipe. The long list of ingredients and steps made me think of the mess still to be made and cleaned up. I began to grill her, and things went downhill quickly.

"What recipe did you base this on? Are you sure the ratios are correct? You know you're going to have to clean this all up, right? Why did you use the farm eggs instead of the store ones?" My voice grew louder, sharper, and belittling. I looked up from the batter and spills to see my daughter's face. Her smile was gone, and she had steeled herself to fight back. I stopped talking, knowing I had failed *again*.

This was not the first time we have fought this battle. My creative daughter loves to bake, and to some degree this is an interest we have fostered together. I knew I should guide her patiently, but even when the two of us do not fight, a battle wages within me.

Internally, I alternate between my maternal love and my selfish nature. I want to support my daughter's interests, her creativity, her personal growth, and the development of her skills. But I also want a clean kitchen, because when she bakes, inevitably, I will have to wipe up the cocoa powder or put away a stray dish. And I want to spend my money carefully because butter and baking chocolate do not come cheap. Plus, I don't really even like cake, so couldn't she at least make a pie?

Most of all, I want to avoid the entire situation by never allowing her to bake so I can pretend to be a good mom and Christian all the time. My delightful, talented daughter is trying to grow into the woman God designed her to be, and I want to eat pie and hide behind a lie.

In this week's scripture reflection, Jesus asked His followers, "If you love those who love you, what credit is that to you?" (Luke 6:32). Jesus cuts to that heart of what or who we love most. He probes into our motivations for doing good. In the midst of the battle between my love for my daughter and my desire for a clean kitchen, the devil would have me believe that I really do love my comfort most, but I know that is not true. And even when I lose that battle in certain moments, the fact that I struggle shows that my heart is working toward being rightly ordered.

Our Lord is calling all of us to examine how we treat those around us. Are we kind and generous? Are we forgiving and patient? If we are good only to those we love (or only when those we love are being good!), that is not enough. Jesus wants us to love our enemies and serve our family members, even when they irritate us.

The catch, of course, is that we cannot do this on our own. We can only love well if we love as God loves, and we can only love like Him if we know Him intimately and deeply. Standing in my messy kitchen, I love Jesus and my daughter best when I look at her and see Him in disguise. And there, in the heart of my home, the King of my heart loves me so that I may love others.

READING: LUKE 6:32–34

- Does anyone in your life present a challenge for you to grow in your capacity for kindness and love? A sister? A neighbor? A coworker? Offer a prayer for her or him today.

- Sometimes we'd rather appear to be behaving like a Christian than actually continue to offer our hearts to Our Lord for reshaping in love. How does this tendency crop up in your life?

WE CAN ONLY
LOVE WELL IF WE
LOVE AS GOD LOVES.

BONNIE ENGSTROM

SERVING MY CALLING

OTHERS-CENTERED

We sat at a long table, each of us surrounded by our own little grouping of detailed notes, to-do lists, and timelines. Having worked hard in anticipation of the meeting, we had come prepared to cross things off our lists and make significant planning progress for our upcoming event.

As each committee chair shared the results of her research, the rest of us asked questions, looked over samples, and offered feedback and support. We then made our recommendation and turned to the ministry's director, Brea, for the approval or direction we needed to proceed.

Thoughtfully, Brea tilted her head and gathered her long brown hair in her hands. "I need to think about it," she said with a warm smile. "I'll have a response to you by the end of the week." But at the end of the week, she didn't have an answer for anyone. We just received an email explaining that yet *another* situation had arisen in her family. With it would be *another* reminder that she needed to put her family first and *another* admonishment that we all needed to put family first.

It was beyond frustrating. As a group, we were composed of single working women all the way to retired grandmothers. Our work had been done during lunch breaks, late nights, and nap times. We were gladly giving our time, talent, and more to a ministry we believed in, but our calendars were full with work, family, and other obligations. Every time Brea missed a deadline, she forced the rest of us to put *her* family first to the detriment of our own families and personal commitments.

I have a desire to serve. This is deeply rooted in me, a genuine yearning to serve the Lord and spread His gospel through serving others and the works of mercy. In fact, baptized Christians share in the roles of priest, prophet, and king, so the wish to be an active part of my community has deep roots in the sacrament of baptism and its indelible mark on my soul.

But I also know that God has given me a primary vocation and a specific calling, and it is through them that God wants me to first love and serve. Brea's execution was off, but her intentions and message were completely accurate. God wanted her to put her family first. God wanted me to put my family first. For her, that meant focusing on her kids; for me, it was spending quality time with my parents, brother, and fiancé.

How do we know what the Lord has called us to? Well, in this week's scripture passage, Jesus told us, "'You shall love the Lord your God with all your heart, and with all your soul, and with all your mind.' This is the greatest and first commandment.

And a second is like it: 'You shall love your neighbor as yourself'" (Matthew 22:37–39). Right here is the answer.

The first part of every day should be saying yes to God. *Yes, I will love You with every bit of myself. Yes, I will turn to You in prayer throughout the day. Yes, I choose You.* And when we get off track, we can turn back to Him and say yes again. We try to complicate discernment, but when we stay close to the Lord, we are already doing His will.

We then turn to the people in our lives—those right in front of us—our families, patients, students, and clients, and we say yes to them. *Yes,* I will help you, comfort you, love you. *Yes,* I will see Christ in you.

We will love better when we love God first, thoroughly, and well. From there we can love others and serve our calling.

READING: MATTHEW 22:37–39

- Who or what is in front of you that you can say yes to while maintaining your peace?
- Do you overcomplicate discernment, thinking somewhere far-off you can be this amazing woman who serves everyone, but in your life here and now you recoil at the present opportunities? Bring this to God.

NEEDING MORE

NEGLECTING SELF-CARE

I shut the front door firmly behind me. Snow blew hard and thick. The wind howled in my face, and I roared back at it. I breathed deeply and slowly, trying to unclench my teeth, fists, shoulders, and back. Every long exhale helped, and eventually my heartbeat steadied. The fury inside me had calmed, but in its absence came an even greater storm of exhaustion. A sob burst through, and my body crumbled against the yellow siding of my front porch.

Inside my home was a crying baby in the crib, a toddler with special needs, and two more small children who wanted and needed me. They wanted me to hold them, help them, read to them, play with them, and soothe them. They needed me to clean them, feed them, protect them, and direct them. Even though I wanted to, I had nothing left to give them.

I had run out of my home and into a blizzard because, for a single moment, I needed to get away from my life. I needed to collect myself in the quiet. On that day, in that season of my life, the closest I could get to quiet was in the bitter cold, my face pelted with snow.

Truly, I was living my lifelong dream: a happily married stay-at-home mom. What I needed to escape were my perceived failures. The laundry was perpetually undone. Unused diapers littered the carpet. Fruit snack wrappers were everywhere. The TV was on non-stop. My clothes didn't fit, and I smelled like sour breast milk.

I thought that my at-home life would be filled with crafts and well-behaved children. I thought I would be thin and the house would be clean with dinner ready at five o'clock. I did not know that I would suffer from undiagnosed perinatal mood and anxiety disorder. Now, a decade later, I can see how unrealistic my standard of effortless perfection was, but in the middle of it, I didn't understand why I was falling so short. The feeling of overwhelming disappointment all day long wears you down. For me, I was left teetering on feelings of hopelessness, seeking refuge in a literal snowstorm.

Sound familiar? A prolonged season where life is demanding without the care for yourself that you need to live it well? A situation where the pain is so unrelenting that you never allow yourself to discern the difference between a cross you can carry and an unrealistic expectation not from the Lord?

Yet Our Creator knows what we need. He calls us to do good work in our vocations, and then He calls us to rest. In this week's scripture for reflection, Jesus said to His disciples, "Come away to a deserted place all by yourselves and rest a while" (Mark 6:31). The disciples had been traveling, praying over people, and anointing the sick. They must have worked long, hard days. And people kept coming to them wanting to be held, helped, soothed, cleaned, fed, protected, and directed.

The Lord saw how much the disciples were giving, so He invited them to rest because He knew we were not created to live in a perpetual state of burnout. The Lord wants us to be refilled with the restorative peace that comes from rest so we can love and serve again.

When I stood out in that winter storm, I was seeking rest, but I needed more. For me, restoration began with medical treatment and the graces of the sacraments. It continues with Adoration, Scripture, prayer, and time spent with loved ones. The tranquility that comes from rest allows us to be present, no matter the storm raging around us.

READING: MARK 6:31

- Consider the storms in your life right now, large or small. Have you taken true rest from the stress they have caused you?
- What refills you? Is it art? Music? Alone time? Time with friends? Adoration? Schedule whatever it is that you need to be refreshed today.

OUR CREATOR
KNOWS WHAT
WE NEED.

BONNIE ENGSTROM

NEW SHOES, NEW ME

PRACTICING SELF-CARE

The pain was sharp. It began on the side of my foot and shot up my leg. I knew it was caused by my cute, deep-pink sneakers. Purchased a few weeks earlier, they were supposed to support me through errands, chores, and tending to the kids. They were failing.

I tried to get through my chores, shifting from foot to foot for momentary relief, but eventually I had to give up. I grimaced as I walked to the living room, pausing to kick off my shoes before dropping to the sofa. I began to gingerly massage the tender spots.

"Buy new shoes," said my husband. I tried to argue with him, but he cut me off. "Bonnie," he said firmly, "you need new shoes. You can have new shoes." He walked down the hall and returned with cash and instructions to leave immediately for a local running shoe store where they would scan and assess my wide, low-arched feet.

It felt luxurious, almost to the point of being ridiculous. But by the time I had returned home, my whole body felt better. Never before had I known the glory of a properly fitted sneaker, and it wasn't luxurious. It was a basic need well met.

Self-care in American culture usually means indulgence beyond our means. But it *should* mean meeting our actual needs in an appropriate way. A pedicure is fun, a treat we can enjoy. But saving the money and taking the time to buy a proper pair of footwear is true self-care that acknowledges the dignity of the human person by meeting a real need.

The lesson was a game changer. Before, I would shift from thinking, *I don't deserve nice things* to *I do not have all the things I so obviously deserve* in a moment. But now I fight to keep the righteous middle ground where my feet are planted firmly in the Lord's definition of who I am.

Self-care is not about what you and I deserve. It's about the worth we have as children of God, created in His image and redeemed by Our Lord Jesus Christ. We are worthy of care and the time, attention, and money that go into properly seeing to our needs.

In this week's scripture passage, Jesus reassured His disciples that they were "of more value than many sparrows" (Matthew 10:31). With confidence He told them, and He tells all of us now, that the Father knows and cares about what happens to even the sparrows. And then, with much tenderness, He explains that we are all far more precious to God than those sparrows.

Of course, the Lord wants our needs to be cared for. Our Creator and heavenly Father has formed us with dignity and asks us to love and respect ourselves in light of that fact. Acts of real self-care are about doing what we need to thrive.

We women are marvelous at putting ourselves last and finding excuses to ignore our needs, and we justify this behavior by claiming we're dying to ourselves or offering something up. However, the Lord may be asking us to do the very opposite of this. It may be that self-care is what we need to do His will for our lives. My new sneakers allowed me to care for my family much better.

Remember the sparrows and how much the Lord loves us. Let's treat ourselves accordingly.

READING: MATTHEW 10:31

- Does self-care feel self-indulgent? Is there an area of your life where you need to care for yourself but haven't made the time because you feel guilty?
- Think about someone who has been an example of treating herself or you with dignity. What did that look like and feel like?

RESENTMENT OVERDONE

COMMUNICATING FROM WOUNDS

The college students' laughter carried across the rec room. I looked up to see them sitting and laughing together while I, their mom-away-from-home, worked alone, wiping down the large table, collecting stray crumbs as I went. I had begun meal prep for the delicious stew and made-from-scratch biscuits hours ago, well before they had come to their home away from home for our family-style dinner. I had worked all afternoon chopping, searing, mixing, and baking, making do with dull knives and wonky cookware the entire time. I had set the table, served the food, washed the dishes, swept the floor, and now—with aching feet and back—I was almost done.

As I circled the kitchen island, a sophomore approached me. He was insecure, but his confidence had been growing through the nurturing friendships he had made at the Catholic student center where I worked. With a twinkle in his eye, he leaned over the counter and asked his "favorite campus minister" to bake some cookies.

I sighed, took a breath, and sharply reminded him about the delicious dinner I had just made. I glared at his stunned friends while I complained about the hours of work I'd done. I narrowed my eyes and told everyone that I was *done* as I stormed out the door.

After huffing away the anger, embarrassment settled in. The students had not been ungrateful. As each one had arrived for the weekly dinner, he or she had cheerfully mentioned how good dinner smelled. They all had beamed at the biscuits and teasingly prophesied that someday I'd win a man's heart with my culinary skills. They had told me it was delicious and thanked me for making it. At any point I could have asked for help, and they would have pitched in. Now I needed to ask them for forgiveness.

When I was younger, I was made to feel that my work and I were not appreciated. This happened in a variety of ways, words said and actions done that chipped away at my feelings of accomplishment and importance. It was an old wound even then.

The Lord and I have spent so much time working on healing that one spot. The Holy Spirit has brought light to the lies and healing graces to the scar tissue. But the wound can reopen with exhaustion and jealousy, producing a shameful bitterness within me. Should anyone get too close to the tender spot, I lash out, as my poor campus ministry family witnessed that night.

Sometimes I feel like the disciples in this week's scripture passage. I come to the Lord and ask Him, "Why am I not yet well? Why do I still need healing? Why do I return to this old scab? Why do I pick at it and open it up again and again? Why can I not be rid of it forever?" Jesus said to the disciples (and says to me now), "Those who are well have no need of a physician, but those who are sick; I have come to call not the righteous but sinners" (Mark 2:17). My healing, and yours, is a gift from Jesus, but He comes to not only heal our wound once. He comes to help us with our scar tissue of sin, to heal us from the inside out.

Faith in Jesus, and confessing our sins, changes even those sins that seem too deeply rooted, the pain too interwoven. But with faith in Jesus, we may be healed, forgiven, and made new.

READING: MARK 2:17

- Have you struggled with loved ones when old wounds resurfaced? Can you first forgive yourself and then turn to them vulnerably to ask for forgiveness?
- Where have you seen growth in your ability to communicate with patience and kindness? Celebrate that and thank God for His grace to continue striving to live that way.

THE LORD COMES
TO HEAL US FROM
THE INSIDE OUT.

BONNIE ENGSTROM

STEADY IN THE STORM

COMMUNICATING FROM LOVE

A sudden, cool wind swooped through the neighborhood, and in a matter of minutes, dark clouds covered the afternoon sun. Animals and people ran for cover as the thunder boomed, lightning struck, and fat raindrops gushed from the sky. Partly scary and partly frustrating, the sudden shift in atmosphere created a fight-or-flight frenzy, and I rushed my kids inside and closed the windows.

If you've ever experienced one of those crazy pop-up summer storms, you'll understand what it's like when my son has a panic attack. Instead of noticing a shift in barometric pressure, I'll see the look on his face, and in a moment everything changes. His big, blue-gray eyes brim with fat crocodile tears that roll down his freckled cheeks. His jaw tightens, and his whole body tenses. If we are out in the world, he may talk back, but at home with just his family, he will roar or scream or crumble into a sobbing pile. Usually all three.

Sometimes it's maddening and sometimes it's frustrating, but mostly it's heartbreaking. Even after years of living through my son's wild panic attacks, I still feel shaken each time they happen. Each one is a different kind of storm, but they all create a fight-or-flight frenzy within me.

I don't want to "batten down the hatches" against him, and I try to meet his tempests with the calm grace he deserves. His counselor gave my husband and me tips on how to help him through his anxiety, and we work hard to follow the wisdom we have gathered.

When I see that look cross his face, I try to stop the attack before it begins. I hug or sit with him. We discuss our plans. We talk through the ways he's safe and does not have to be afraid. We review everything again. If I see his anxiety spike, I ask if he needs a break or I help him find his words to communicate how he feels. And if the panic attack comes anyway, we shift to a different gear.

I wish you could see my husband and the way he chooses to love in the face of terrible screams and hurtful words. He exudes a tangible strength, tempered with gentleness, and his steady, smooth voice walks through the questions and answers our son needs. He is patient and kind, not quick-tempered. He does not tolerate certain lines being crossed, but he is merciful.

We all fail at times. Our children, friends, family, and the Lord know that we fail. In our daily challenges, we lose our tempers; we lose our cool. But the Lord invites us to try again. For me, it takes courage to enter into a hard situation, but fueled by my love for our son, I will always enter this storm.

What storms are you entering? Which crosses are you carrying? When the Lord allows those we love most to carry heavy crosses, they become ours too. We embrace them together because we trust in the Lord and His promise of peace.

"Peace I leave with you. . . . Do not let your hearts be troubled, and do not let them be afraid," Jesus said to His apostles (John 14:27), and I take His words to heart. When my son's anxiety spikes, I lean into these words. When the storm begins to rage, I breathe them in and out. When things spin out of my control, I focus on His promise, spoken in great love.

Sister, you are given this same assurance. You and your loved ones will never be asked to carry your crosses alone. Remember that Jesus promises, "My peace I give to you" (v. 27).

READING: JOHN 14:27

- Our Lord is with you even, and especially, in the most violent storms of your life. How can you incorporate this promise of His peace into your daily prayer?
- Who in your close circle is suffering right now? Ask the Holy Spirit to help you reach out to them and assure them they aren't alone.

WEEK 35

SHOULDERING
RESPONSIBILITIES

DISCONNECTION

It was just past 8:00 p.m. on Michaelmas, the Feast of the Archangels. It was a school night, and I had just finished tucking my six full-bellied, freshly bathed younger children into bed when my middle schoolers walked through the front door. My husband, whose workday had begun over twelve hours beforehand, walked in behind them. They explained that the cross-country meet went long and then asked for something to eat.

"You were supposed to be home two hours ago," I snapped back. "We waited a half an hour to have dinner with you. I made a whole feast!" I then ranted about our lack of family time before I moved on to belittling the school that didn't have enough volunteers to efficiently run a meet. I sent them to the kitchen for leftovers while loudly reminding them that I hated sports because they—not family, not church, not even school—dictated our schedule and robbed us of already-limited family time.

SHOULDERING RESPONSIBILITIES

Sports were not important in my childhood home, and I saw no need for them to be an integral part of my children's lives. My husband, a coach and former student athlete, disagreed. As he nurtured our kids' sports interests, my resentment grew. With every schedule conflict and sport prioritization, this point of contention grew into an increasingly bigger issue, and my outbursts became more frequent.

Now, my sincerest hope for my kids has always been that they will joyfully love Jesus and His Church for their entire lives. I also pray they will be healthy, make good decisions, and know they are loved. And because of our family dynamics, daily family dinners have been invaluable for meeting these goals.

My husband agrees with me, but he also believes that our family will not suffer if, during various sports seasons, family dinners can only happen several times a week. In fact, he believes that sports and other extracurriculars are an important part of reaching our shared end goal for the kids' lives and souls.

In this week's Gospel reflection, Jesus said, "You will all become deserters; for it is written, 'I will strike the shepherd, and the sheep will be scattered'" (Mark 14:27). But in my grasp for control, I interpreted it as, "Sheep scattered to various ball fields will fall away from their faith, striking the heart of their mom, er, shepherd." This, of course, is not what He meant at all.

Jesus was talking to His disciples, but perhaps His warning is for us too. As a shepherd to my children, I must ascertain what strike will truly disrupt our flock. In this particular instance of my kids playing sports, even though it has meant some chaos in our lives, my single-mindedness had to bend. It was worth it for unity.

Consistently nurturing my kids does not always happen around the dinner table. Instead, it often looks like passing out snacks, water bottles, and encouragement as the older kids leave and then welcoming them home with excited interest and a warm meal. Usually, it means joyfully caring for the little ones still at home. Occasionally, it means bringing my entire family to an event so we can all cheer on the ones who are competing. And it always includes sharing these responsibilities with my husband when he's home, and joyfully shouldering them alone when his coaching schedule takes him elsewhere.

Perhaps you also find your rigidity inhibiting growth in the lives of those you love. Consider if your stubborn insistence that life aligns with your vision is prohibiting growth in your own heart. Now entrust your schedule, your family, and your vision to the Shepherd.

No matter how far our kids or other loved ones have scattered or may scatter, He will help us love well and fill in the places where we are lacking.

READING: MARK 14:27

- What stressor in your schedule would you like to entrust to the Good Shepherd right now?
- Are you being rigid when you could be flexible and still pursue unity with your loved ones? Be honest with yourself.

GOD WILL
HELP US
LOVE WELL.

BONNIE ENGSTROM

THE HOLY WORK TOGETHER

CONNECTION

We stood before our freshly tilled garden plot, the late spring sun shining cheerfully in the afternoon sky. Throughout the morning, we pulled weeds, cleared clutter, and gathered tools and seeds. Now, with full bellies and fresh sunblock, my children each held a packet of seeds for their own special crop—carrots, beans, popcorn, and more. It was time to plant.

Standing in bare feet and measuring with small hands, my kids pushed seeds into the supple soil. My sons used shovels and toy dump trucks to form mounds of dirt for the squash. My girls carefully labeled each row. My husband put up a fence to keep out the bunnies, and I put down straw to block the weeds. As we worked, we imagined the salads and salsas our garden would supply and predicted how many jack-o'-lanterns and pies the pumpkins would produce.

Dinner was a picnic of sandwiches and apples, eaten beneath

our shade tree. Then, as the shadows lengthened and the sky became golden pink and indigo, we went inside to scrub away the dirt and settle down for a family movie night. Between rolls of laughter, the kids ate handfuls of popcorn, and my husband and I locked eyes and smiled.

We were tired, but deeply satisfied. Family dynamics can be difficult, but on that day we pulled together to fulfill a shared vision. We worked hard and took turns. We shared and discovered earthworms and roly-polies. We discussed the water cycle and the difference between a spade and a shovel. There was bickering and there was complaining, but overwhelmingly it was a day of companionship and unity. Everyone participated; everyone had a role.

The planting of the garden, and the daily work of tending to it over the following weeks and months, was part of a larger goal shared by my husband and me. Namely, we love the Lord and want our children to love Him too. We want to foster a family culture that marvels at the world and praises God for His creativity. We want our children to understand that growth happens in silence, and weeds (and sin) take over if not regularly tended to. My husband and I want our kids to understand that healthy plants are sometimes thinned out or cut back so they yield a higher quantity and quality of produce.

Ultimately, our goal for them is heaven.

Hopefully, you've also experienced the vibrancy of being part of a family, group, or community that successfully works together toward a shared goal. Such healthy relationships are gifts from God, and He models them for us in the early Church.

In this week's scripture we read, "The whole group of those

who believed were of one heart and soul, and no one claimed private ownership of any possessions, but everything they owned was held in common" (Acts 4:32). The early Church had a shared goal—to know, love, and serve the Lord and to preach the Good News of Jesus Christ to the ends of the earth. They came together in agreement, sharing what they had and combining their gifts to meet their goal. Surely there were tough times, but they obviously worked through them—we know they were successful.

If there is a lack of unity in your family relationships or family life, take it to the Lord. Invite Him to review the situation and give you the needed grace to address the issues. Sit down with your loved ones and begin the holy work of coming together so that, for the glory of the Lord and your good, your family may be "of one heart and soul" with "everything . . . in common."

READING: ACTS 4:32

- In your life, who has been an example of this kind of family unity—not because they are perfect but because they're willing to communicate? What lessons can you take away from them?
- Draft a prayer for unity with your loved ones today. Bring them to Jesus' Sacred Heart for healing. How do you want to begin?

PART FIVE

YOUR
RELATIONSHIP
WITH FRIENDS

SARAH ERICKSON

Let us take this time to ask ourselves: *How do those around me reinforce or impact my identity as God's beloved daughter?*

Friends provide the incredible gift of knowing another person and being known by him or her. These relationships change our lives. In this section, we'll walk through eight stories from my life—in contrasting pairs. I'll share interdependence and independence in friendship, peer pressure and peer leadership, poor and powerful examples of friendship, and lost and restored friendships. I encourage you to open your Bible and follow along. Take time with the questions and let them sit inside your heart.

UNWANTED AND UNWELCOME

FAULTY IDENTITY

From my seat on the floor, I investigated the pattern of the dirtied paper plates scattered around the elegantly furnished living room. I shifted my attention from the plates to the circle of men surrounding me, each sitting in his designated chair, and wondered if they noticed me on the rug below. After all, I had only secured my place on the corner of the rug by way of the "girlfriend pity invite." There was one other woman in the room, and she sat poised on an armrest, in all of her belonging as a wife.

I studied each of their faces—they were lost in a discussion about philosophy well beyond me—and took note of their grand collective. They each had mastered the ability to speak without really encountering the person he was speaking to and to stand next to someone without being close to him. I longed to lock eyes with one of them and for him to ask me what I thought, but no one did.

The Aristotelian debate waged on around me. How was I embedded in a friend group that did not understand me? My then boyfriend and his philosophy buddies always gathered in an intellectual space I was not invited to, and one I realized I did not wish to enter. The exclusion I experienced at the hand of these "intellectuals" steadily reinforced false ideas about my identity. I desperately wanted this group to care for me and be curious about me, and when they didn't and weren't, I subsequently blamed myself for being lonely on the corner rug.

Since I do not feel comfortable, I must be irrational. Since they do not ask questions, my story must be unremarkable. Since I am on the floor, I must be unwanted and unwelcome. Since I feel lonely, I must be overly emotional. These lies dictated my narrative for so long that I forgot what my own experience was. It took being fully rejected by this friend group to start excavating the roots of these premises and to start asking why I had allowed the exclusive behavior of others to place doubt on the worth of my story.

After all, my story is worthwhile.

Perhaps there is an instance in which someone made you feel as though your presence was not important or wanted. Perhaps you have taken on blame for the way others have excluded you. Perhaps you have wrongfully internalized this experience as your identity. Call to mind the full weight of that memory, recalling the lies and the false narrative you adopted about your identity, and ask yourself, Does this experience offer any insight into who I really am?

Sister, your identity as a beloved daughter of God is not contingent on how others treat you. The Lord delights in you and accepts you. He yearns for an eternity with you.

In this week's scripture, Jesus said, "For where your treasure is, there your heart will be also" (Luke 12:34). When we believe lies about who we are—that we are not worthy or do not matter—we choose a treasure that does not feed our hearts. We become familiar with these lies, gripping them tightly in self-defense, thinking they are the truth.

Yet Jesus comes close to you and me and asks us to trade our lies for His life-giving treasure. Jesus offers us nothing short of a forever love. When we choose to bind ourselves to Truth as the ultimate treasure, we find ourselves reconciled with our true identity as the beloved.

Sister, this is the gold worth keeping and where we want our hearts to be.

READING: LUKE 12:34

- Have you felt unseen or unaffirmed by people in your life? Take any instance of this suffering to Our Lord and the Blessed Mother for comfort.
- Forever love is your inheritance. Can you accept this idea that Jesus and God and the Holy Spirit love you beyond your imagination?

JESUS OFFERS US
NOTHING SHORT
OF A FOREVER LOVE.

SARAH ERICKSON

PEACE AND A MILKSHAKE

RESTORED IDENTITY

Sitting in the passenger seat and stuck in the late-night Whataburger drive-thru line, I thought about my early flight the next morning and how I should probably get some sleep. Yet when I looked over and caught the eager expression of my longtime friend, who was picking the next song to play in her car, my worries dissipated. We were just two college graduates, waiting on our Dr. Pepper milkshakes.

In that long drive-thru line, I was delighted to be in her white sedan because we rarely had these times together anymore. Even though she had been my best friend in high school, our friendship had struggled when I moved across the country for school. I had changed radically in college and lost a desire to nurture our friendship, which I had hesitantly vocalized to her. We didn't have an argument or falling-out; rather, the tangible, physical distance led to our relational distance, which I had discovered peace with.

Undoubtedly, the voice of Jesus had led me to new friends in college, but I felt bad about how easy it was to let go of my high school ties. Was it wrong to step into this new life with so much joy, and was it okay to hold new dreams close?

That night, as I reflected on our friendship journey, I found a new peace. Jesus spoke wordlessly in my heart, "Have peace, My child." My old friend and I were able to be present and near to each other, unconcerned with the time we had spent apart and the time we would spend waiting on milkshakes. I smiled, soaked in the drive-thru's fluorescent light, and listened to her give the full backstory on the song she had just added to the queue.

In that moment, I was thankful my newly discovered peace had carried us from growing apart to a place of connectedness, simply together and grateful for it. The moment of reunion with Paige reminded me that I did not have to figure it all out. All that had led up to that cherished Dr. Pepper milkshake was sustained by the sweet hands of Jesus, teaching me that redemption in a relationship is real and mine to hold.

Perhaps you have experienced a similar distance with a friend or family member. Maybe you have been apart for years, or maybe the Lord's steady hand has led you to grow back together. These experiences can make us feel anxious to put all the pieces together as the perfect orchestrator. However, in all of our shifting, the Lord calls us to "strive first for the kingdom of God and his righteousness" (Matthew 6:33).

This kingdom calling is the most liberating burden-lifter in a complicated relationship. When we sit with this command, we realize that we are allowed to put aside our anxieties and refocus on the Lord's call. When we soak in this message, we reclaim our stories.

When we put the Kingdom of God first, before all of our friendships, Scripture tells us that all these things will be given to us as well. Sister, the Lord wants to take care of us and tend to our friendships. When we follow His peace and stay locked into His wisdom, the Lord offers us full relationships wherein He provides for all our needs. When we find we cannot be present in friendship, when we cannot provide, the Lord fills in the gaps with His kindness.

I am so awestruck by the way the Lord has redeemed my friendship and breathed new life into it. Let us allow this scripture to heal wide disconnects and move us to gratitude.

READING: MATTHEW 6:33

- Are you struggling with a friendship that has shifted or changed? Take a moment to examine the connection and probe into your heart if you need to reach out in love.
- Our Lord wants to redeem our broken relationships. Celebrate a healed relationship you've experienced today. How did that take place?

LIFE LIVED FOR JESUS

PEER PRESSURE

The sunlit house reeked of teenage angst and excitement, scattered with evidence of a Catholic high school graduating class ringing in the soon-to-be freedom of college. As I stood there, I realized my invitation to this party was some cruel joke where my classmates had invited the token "Jesus freak" to watch her squirm.

I scanned the room for an ally or maybe a rock to hide under and locked eyes with the person I wanted to hide from the most. He sprawled on the couch with several girls across his lap and asked, "What would Jesus think about you drinking that beer?" The girls snickered; I blushed.

I had only taken a few sips of the beer in my hand. I responded, "I don't know—but I do know that I do not actually want to be here, and there's so much more to life than this. I know I will not regret choosing a life with Jesus, and that in the end your opinion won't matter."

My monologue was cut short. I was escorted out, but I did not look back.

I suppose my reason for attending the party was to prove that I could be the "youth group" girl and still secure approval from a select group of boys who had taunted me throughout high school for my faith. I figured if I carried the right props (that is, beer), they would admit I was worthy of a special place in that room. I thought I could prove my way into acceptance. I wanted both the way of Jesus and the way of the world, and I wanted to be comfortably liked somewhere in the middle.

Yet that middle road never happened because I had firmly chosen Jesus. The freedom of His friendship enabled me to speak about the life Jesus had promised me—more to be desired than any fleeting moment of high school popularity. I was relieved to have been excluded because it confirmed in me that the substance of my life was real. My life was about the gospel. In the end, I gave up dreams of sitting next to a dismissive boy and embraced a lifetime of belonging and closeness with Jesus.

Sister, can you remember a moment when you wanted to be included, only to realize it was not fulfilling?

Sometimes, in our longing to be included, we forget we are already included by God. This reaching for recognition can pull us into destructive behavior, particularly when we seek it from those who do not honor our divinely ordained dignity. Matthew 5:30 reminds us that it is better to lose what causes us to sin than to lose ourselves entirely.

When you and I are tempted to hide from our identity as daughters of the Father, He is closer than ever, asking us to let go of our worldly attachments. He is near us in the humiliating space of peer pressure, offering us refuge and a new life. The life we find on the other side of all that we let go of is offered to us by a Father who does not pressure us or mock us. For all the times we have tried to prove we deserve a seat at the table, He has already offered us one.

From this seat, our interior safe haven, we are secured in a lasting love that allows us to face exclusion with the confidence that we are already chosen. There is no regret in choosing a life lived with Jesus.

READING: MATTHEW 5:30

- Think about a time when you felt crushed by peer pressure. Was there an ally by your side? Walk through that memory with Our Lord, who will protect you all along the way.
- Who have you seen pull a chair out for someone to join others at a table? What lesson did you learn from that, and how can you include others more intentionally in your circles?

THERE IS NO
REGRET IN CHOOSING
A LIFE LIVED WITH JESUS.

SARAH ERICKSON

WEEK 40

LEADING WITH INTEGRITY

PEER LEADERSHIP

I nervously watched my feet dangle from the wobbling bar stool. I let it distract me from the disapproving looks of my professor and classmates, who were taking turns bashing the Church's teachings on sexual morality, until I spoke up and subsequently heard, "Come on. You don't seriously believe in all that stuff. I thought I respected you."

My professor's accusatory tone cut through the pub's hazy air like a lighthouse beam. It stung to watch his eyebrows furrow when I asserted that I did not find the Church's sexual ethics restrictive, but instead liberating. The tension made me feel as if I was swearing off women's progress by choosing to pursue chastity.

I considered whether I should simply lie and pretend I did not abide by the Church's teachings; after all, he had not graded my final exam yet. Not a soul in all of central London would come to my rescue now, not even any of my Catholic classmates.

"I do believe in all that stuff. Even when it feels hard to." I cleared my throat.

All at once, everyone around the table reacted like a mob holding up vitriol instead of torches.

When I walked out of the pub that night, I knew that I would definitely see the consequences for my Catholic witness on my final grade. My professor had made it clear he did not respect my stance or beliefs. It was not until my flight back to the US weeks later that I received his comments on my final paper.

I'm a wee bit of a cynic, and I was beginning to suspect that genuine integrity was as extinct as the dodo; your conviction and faith, however, gave me a real shock when it dawned on me during our final meeting that yours was the real deal. You may not be a dodo, but you are a rare bird.

The astonishment I felt still dwells on the inside of me, continuing to teach me that witnessing to the Truth is always worthwhile. Even if my surrounding community responds with hostility, I can rest knowing my calling is to the Truth. "Conviction" and "faith"—these words have empowered me to rebuke even attractive lies when I hear them. Sister, which of your communities, whether familial, academic, professional, or even spiritual, need to be redirected toward the gospel?

In today's scripture, Jesus reminded the disciples, "If the world hates you, be aware that it hated me before it hated you" (John 15:18). He knew what they would face in His name, and He knows what you and I face now. In a way, the mockery at standing up for my faith was actually a moment to embrace my chosenness, as He has "chosen [me] out of the world" (v. 19).

When my faith is mocked, it *is* painful. In response, I can easily begin to question whether I am naïve, and it can feel like a threat to the goodness of my story.

Questions about my worth swirled around in my brain as I left that pub meeting with my class. It would have felt vindicating to respond with similar hostility, eviscerating my peers in an intellectual battle. Yet when my professor admitted he may have been too quick to criticize me, I allowed Jesus to let it soften me. I allowed it to be a moment of Him calling me His own.

Instead of burying myself in consolation that I was right all along, I allowed my heart to be drenched in humility, so that by the Spirit's aid I could offer a glimmer of hope to my cynical professor.

In these moments when our faith is tested, we have an opportunity to illuminate dimly lit spaces with love and confidence.

READING: JOHN 15:17–19

- Have you experienced an awkward moment of witnessing to your faith in front of your peers? Consider the courage it took to do it, even imperfectly, and offer a prayer of thanksgiving for God's help.
- Who has witnessed to you in humility and love through words or actions? Thank God for her or him now.

WITNESS TO LOVE

POOR EXAMPLE

With a long drive ahead of me, I hit play on my favorite reality TV star's podcast, with hopes of being entertained. I decided to listen to one of his dating episodes where he took calls from listeners, diagnosed their issues, and advised them accordingly. As I cruised down the highway, I sipped my latte and braced myself for an hour and a half of relationship turmoil, despite it not being my usual content of choice.

My interest took a new direction when I heard the humanity in the first caller's pained tone as she described how her boyfriend of several years had mistreated her. Despite all of it, she longed to make it work, and I let out a sigh as my heart broke for her kindred, hopeful heart.

I was somewhat alarmed at the star's response as he berated her, calling her desperate, dumb, and delusional. His reaction was insensitive, masked as "just being honest," and I soon realized he offered no advice outside of, "Have fewer feelings." Suddenly, the distortion of reality TV touched reality, at least for me, and it was no longer distantly entertaining, but personally harmful.

I quickly turned the podcast off.

Soon after, I stopped following this influencer on Instagram and stopped listening to his podcast because his lack of compassion toward these hurting women normalized a worldview with which I do not align.

During the months I listened to this influencer's content, the way he spoke tore women down in their time of confusion and turned it into entertainment, and it subtly translated into an attitude of pride for me. When women in my life would share their own woundedness with me, I found myself being critical and harsh, asserting myself above them. With this mindset, I embraced gossip and hardened my heart against those longing for connection.

The podcast moment showed me I did not desire to be treated that way in my own hurt. In fact, if I was vulnerable and spoken to so insensitively, it would only compound my grief. The empathy I felt in that moment sent me on a journey of seeking out people in my life, both in my immediate community and on social media, who had been hurt by my hardened heart.

Sister, is someone in your life setting an example that influences you to treat others in a way you would not want to be treated? These poor examples of love contradict the way scripture calls us to love. In this week's scripture we hear, "Do to others as you would have them do to you" (Luke 6:31). This verse is a call for me to love in a way I would want to be loved, despite what I may hear from a worldly influencer. It calls us to a holy awareness of our witness of love, in the way we both receive and give it, and gives us a taste of the Love who was first breathed into us.

In our relationships with others, we can be tempted to allow poor examples to disintegrate the way we live securely as daughters of the Father. Yet we reaffirm our commitment to our greatest Love by choosing to love others as we would hope to be loved—with compassion, kindness, and gentleness. As we love others in obedience to the gospel's call, we communicate God's love to all His children.

READING: LUKE 6:31

- Who has loved you well? From whom have you learned to love others well? What does that look like in the story of your life?
- Remember a time someone mocked your pain or ridiculed you for a particular response to your situation. Now forgive that person, letting God's love wash over you.

LET'S REAFFIRM
OUR COMMITMENT
TO OUR GREATEST LOVE.

SARAH ERICKSON

HEALED BY LISTENING

POWERFUL EXAMPLE

Perched on a log in the Potomac River, I sensed a heaviness in my body. Like the air, heavy with moisture, my spirits were weighed down. A new friend of mine who had just moved to DC had driven me to this quaint waterfall spot, where she asked me about my experience of community after college. As I responded, I could hear the disappointment in my once-hopeful tone, and all the loneliness packed into my answer: "I do not really ever feel understood." Truly, I unraveled for several hours as I shared about how I dreamed of a female community where I felt received and a space where I could pray in a way that was expressive, creative, and musical.

My friend listened to me completely from start to finish, and by the safety of our exchange, I knew she understood me. On the mud-coated log we shared, she asked if we could pray and discern what it would mean to create the community we so desperately hoped for. She offered to walk alongside me, accompanying me in my loneliness, and then catalyzed a vision for community I would not have seen as possible.

I did not have the fortitude to harness my loneliness and recast it as an opportunity for community-building, but my kind, holy friend did, and my life is radically different for it. If I had never shared my loneliness with her that day in such trust and vulnerability, I would not have gone on to start a worship ministry for young adults at my diocese or hosted a Blessed Brunch[1] the following month to connect women in my neighborhood. By her example and with her companionship, I am learning to make an offering of my life and have leaned into the deep connectedness that offers.

Sister, we should all have someone who shows up for us as my friend did and reminds us what it looks like to pursue heaven's treasure. Who is that woman for you? Perhaps it is a friend from college or a woman at your parish. Maybe it is a woman at your place of work or in your neighborhood, or maybe you are several time zones away. The deep work of listening and encouraging each other takes place in these kinds of friendships. It is here we are empowered to go forth from one another and create space for others.

Understanding our lives as offerings not only nourishes our communities, but it serves the Kingdom. It is the call put on our hearts by Jesus, as heard in this week's scripture: "Sell your possessions, and give alms. Make purses for yourselves that do not wear out, an unfailing treasure in heaven, where no thief comes near and no moth destroys" (Luke 12:33). We are called to offer not only our possessions but ourselves.

---

1. Learn more at blessedisshe.net/blessed-brunches.

Our friendships with women must reconvict us of a desire to live wholly devoted to Jesus where we are always aligned with our identity as beloved. When we help each other pursue heaven, loving others as Jesus would, we create communities that endure forever. By creating space for each other, by listening and praying together, we might be integral in another's healing and growth.

Since my friend lives her life this way, she was free to offer me hours of uninterrupted, agenda-free time on that log, fully able to receive me, much as I imagine Jesus would have. And it is still ministering to me over a year later.

READING: LUKE 12:33

- Run through a list of women in your life you would like to give intentional time to. How is God asking you to make space for each one? Reach out today.
- Are you part of a community that feeds you? What would you change about your friend group or relationships to make sure they feed you spiritually as well as emotionally?

BEST FRIEND BETRAYAL

FRIENDSHIP LOST

I stared at my tear-filled eyes as I sat cross-legged in front of my bedroom's dusty mirror, avoiding the checklist of assignments for my junior year of high school. I despised how the light of my phone reflected the mascara smeared all over my blemish-covered cheeks, but most of all, I despised how I had allowed my best friend to make me feel so abandoned.

Earlier that night, in the church parking lot, my first love, whom I had spent about a year trying to make into my first boyfriend, told me my best friend had confessed her undying feelings for him. He had decided to pursue her instead of me. My cheeks had abruptly reddened in rage. Sure, I knew boys broke hearts, but I had no idea best friends did.

I gazed down at my manicured thumbs, hovering over the blank text message I had yet to write. Our friendship was lost in its current form no matter what my fifteen-year-old self typed.

"I feel so lied to. I feel betrayed." I hit Send, hoping for an admission of wrongdoing or a sign of remorse. Neither came.

I wailed from my core into the night, grieving the loss of the friend who knew me best.

Reflecting back on it now, this friend was the first friend to invite me into the Church, and, because of that, her friendship was deeply impactful for my formation. I trusted her as I would have trusted a sister. She had chosen to discard our connection for a temporary relationship, which was incredibly wounding and disorienting.

Even now, as an adult, I can see how that loss had hardening effects on my heart, planting seeds of cynicism about experiences of community. For years, I longed for reconciliation in that friendship, but even after her short-lived relationship with the boy I liked, she never attempted to regain my trust or rebuild our friendship. That rejection hurt more than the betrayal.

Sister, it is deeply painful when we entrust friends with our hearts and we are rejected, or when our care for them is not fully reciprocated. We can carry these wounds from childhood all the way into our adult lives, where the echoes of past hurts are heard in different kinds of losses in different seasons. Each loss adds to the wound and provokes questions about our belonging, not only in our communities, but in the eyes of Our Father.

As we mourn our lost friendships, we grapple with our inner void and the lie that we are alone, abandoned, lost. Yet in this week's scripture, we hear, "For the Son of Man came to seek out and to save the lost" (Luke 19:10).

As we stand in the depths of our grief and cry out from our seemingly unloved, abandoned place, we are in the best posture to encounter the One who came to save all that was lost. Only in His incarnation, crucifixion, and resurrection do we find that no friendships are truly lost in Him.

Sister, this does not erase our pain or eliminate our need to grieve. Yet with a Messiah who saves what is lost, who delights in the redemption of our wounds, we find that He reconciles us to Him and redeems our relationships, like the thoughtful Shepherd He is. It has been of immense consolation for me to remember this.

In heaven, a life of broken friendships is redeemed by an eternity of perfect union with God.

READING: LUKE 19:10

- Have you lost an important friendship? Did it go through a season of change, or is it completely behind you? Thank God for the love and lessons that were in it, even if it remains lost or stirs a painful memory.

- In Jesus, everything can be redeemed. If you are unsure about reaching out to a friend with whom you have had a hard time, bring her and the situation to prayer. What do you feel is a prompting of the Holy Spirit?

THE LORD
REDEEMS OUR
RELATIONSHIPS.

SARAH ERICKSON

GOD'S VISION FOR SISTERHOOD

FRIENDSHIP RESTORED

I rolled over in my bed, eyes pierced by the sun coming through the shade, and noticed my roommate hadn't stirred this morning after a party the night before. It stung to watch her rest because my heart was still raw over one silly, offhand comment she had made. I also knew she would be oblivious to my hurt unless I spoke up. I had gone to sleep with the unprocessed hurt, allowing my dreams to be consumed with anxiety, and still awoke with the ache. This ache whispered a pervasive lie: *I must be a burden to her.*

As she woke up and greeted me cheerfully, my heart raced because I knew the call before me was to be honest. I confessed I had not slept well on account of a series of stress-inducing dreams, all provoked by one comment from the night. As I mentioned the comment, she fell into a soft, regretful laugh, and she immediately apologized, "I am so sorry. I did not mean that." Her nonchalant reaction reminded me to breathe and prompted me to release my fear. "That's okay." I smiled back.

As a deeply sensitive person, I had spent much of my life not expressing when my friends had hurt my feelings because I did not trust that my friendships could endure those tough conversations. I truly doubted whether my friends cared for me enough to stick around when our love called for forgiveness and restoration. Yet in that lighthearted, sunlit moment with my roommate, I was moved by how meaningful restoration is when it is small and simple, instead of being an all-encompassing, dramatic experience that the friendship can't handle.

In fact, I am convinced of the strength a friendship can have because of the way moments like this have taught us to practice forgiveness, allowing it to carry us through regular, honest dialogue about our hurts, instead of deepening and convoluting wounds.

Sister, when was the last time you were able to forgive someone and, because of it, deepen your friendship? Perhaps it was a coworker or a neighbor. Maybe it was even a family member, such as a sister or a sister-in-law. It could have even been your best friend, a friendship that has deepened ever since you chose to forgive her or him.

These instances of forgiveness are worth treasuring because they call us to remember, as daughters, that we can only forgive because we are first forgiven by the Father. We are brought back to this central truth in this week's scripture (Luke 11:4). We first ask the Father to forgive our sins, and then we can forgive those who have sinned against us.

These two steps cannot be separated from each other. Our movements toward reconciliation with others are an extension of our identity as daughters, where we are brought in close to the Father and invited to meet Him and experience His compassion. Only then can we begin to practice forgiveness, and not just in catastrophic moments. In the daily moments of friendship, we remember how intimately we are loved first. This Love draws us closer to understanding and tenderness toward one another and creates a space where communion is restored and debts are forgiven.

When we become more aware of our daughterhood and more attuned to how the Father looks at us, we are liberated to be honest with each other and to forgive each other because restoration is His vision for our sisterhood.

READING: LUKE 11:4

- Is regular and honest dialogue a part of your close friendships, even when that dialogue includes conflict or confrontation over miscommunications and hurt feelings? If not, do you wish it were?
- Does forgiveness come easily to you, or do you tend to ruminate over tensions, exacerbating them? Resolve to be direct or let things go today.

PART SIX

YOUR RELATIONSHIP WITH CALLING

EMILY STIMPSON CHAPMAN

Let us take this time to ask ourselves: *How does my work help me give honor and glory to God?*

Our relationship to work and calling is complicated—it's where we spend a majority of our time, it's the people we often see the most, and it can change during different seasons of life. In this section, we'll walk through eight stories from my life—in contrasting pairs—that relate to work and calling. I'll share finding my identity in work and then glorifying God in my work, the pursuit of glory and the pursuit of God, wrongly ordered priorities and rightly ordered priorities, and grudging discernment and prayerful discernment. I encourage you to open your Bible and follow along. Take time with the questions and let them sit inside your heart.

DEFINED BY WHAT I DID

IDENTITY IN WORK

"The Speaker wants you at tonight's meeting."

I stared, confused, at my boss, a US congressman. "The Speaker of the House?"

"What other Speaker is there?" He laughed. "He liked the letter you wrote about the Mexico City policy. He wants more letters before the vote. We'll talk about it in his office tonight."

Hours later, I was walking by my boss's side, the clicking of my three-inch heels echoing through the Capitol's empty corridors.

When we arrived in the Speaker's quarters, a secretary clad in Brooks Brothers pointed us toward the meeting room. Inside, several members of Congress and senior staffers sat waiting. My boss and I grabbed seats near the fireplace, under a painting of some long-dead statesmen. Moments later, the Speaker entered.

"Jim," the Speaker barked. "Where's the staffer who did that letter?"

My boss nodded toward me.

"Can you do two more like that before Thursday?" the Speaker asked. "They'll go out under my signature."

"Yes, sir," I replied. "I'll have something to you before nine a.m."

I bowed my head to hide my smile. I was twenty-two years old, four months out of college, and had just been asked to write for the Speaker of the House.

Over the next eleven months, I moved up through the congressional staff ranks. By age twenty-three, I was the youngest legislative director on Capitol Hill. Everyone expected great things of me. And I worked sixteen hours a day, six days a week in pursuit of that greatness.

But there was a price to pay. As the months passed, my already-thin body grew thinner. The eating disorder I had beaten back in college returned. The more pressure that mounted on me at work, the more controlling I became with food. By August, I was sick with hunger and exhaustion.

It had to stop. I needed to step back and find healing. But that meant walking away from Capitol Hill and from the woman I thought I was: the woman who could do it all, who could get things done faster, better, and more efficiently than anyone else; the woman who didn't fail.

Like so many of us, I had bought in to the lie that what I did and accomplished made me valuable. And the fear that grips us when we find our identity in doing gripped me: If I walked away, who would I be? Would I matter to anyone?

In Saint John's Gospel we read, "But to all who received him, who believed in his name, he gave power to become children of God" (1:12). John is talking about me. And you. And every baptized person. When the baptismal waters were poured over your forehead, God poured His life into your soul, changing you forever, making you not just His creature but His child.

The world doesn't want you to remember that. It wants you to make the mistake I made and find your identity in what you do. It also wants you to believe that the more you do, the more you matter.

To God, though, you matter because you *are*. Before the world existed, He thought of you. He saw you. He delighted in you. He loved you. He loves you still, as you are.

You don't have to work sixteen-hour days to give God glory or to earn God's love. You can't earn it. His love is an unmerited gift. You can receive it or reject it, but no matter what you choose, God will keep loving you. He is your Father. That's what good fathers do.

Hold fast to that truth. We are His. This is our identity.

READING: JOHN 1:12–13

- Have you been tempted to believe you are what you do and how you do it?
- Think about a person who gives you unconditional love in your life: your mom, a boyfriend, a close friend.

BEFORE THE
WORLD EXISTED,
OUR LORD
THOUGHT OF YOU.

EMILY STIMPSON CHAPMAN

ONLY GOD'S APPROVAL

IDENTITY IN GOD

The glowing numbers on the alarm clock changed from 5:29 to 5:30 a.m., and the beeping commenced. I jumped, fumbled, then quickly silenced it, not wanting to wake my roommate.

In the dark, I pulled my red hair into a ponytail, threw on a pair of overalls, then slipped out of my new home, an old chicken coop converted into two small apartments. A windmill rattled in the breeze as I walked across the grass toward the retreat house on the Chesapeake Bay where I now served.

I entered the house, went straight to the kitchen, and set the coffee to brewing.

While I waited, I stepped out onto the deck. The light of the rising sun illuminated the still waters of the bay. I breathed, whispering a prayer of thanks—for the sunrise and water, for the quiet and the day's work awaiting me, and most of all for the joy I had found here.

Two months earlier I had left DC and moved to Maryland's Eastern Shore to volunteer at this Evangelical-owned retreat house. A friend had suggested I come here, thinking it might give me the space I needed to detox from politics and begin to heal.

He was right.

On this particular morning, I had a busy day ahead of me: cook breakfast for the twenty-five guests who had spent the week with us, then, after they left, turn over all the rooms before the next guests arrived. Besides doing the cooking for guests and crew, I would dust baseboards, scour bathtubs, scrub toilets, strip beds, then make beds. If all went well, I might get back to my room before 10:00 p.m.

No one besides my fellow workers would see what I did. No one would praise me for how well I washed the dishes or reward me for how the bathroom faucets shined. This was not the kind of work that the world tells us is important. It wasn't laying a foundation for future financial stability or enhancing my résumé. But I loved it just the same.

For the first time in my life, I was no longer chasing anyone's approval but God's. I worked for Him. I wanted to love and honor our guests. More important, though, I wanted to love and honor Jesus. Working amid the pots, pans, and bedsheets, I'd found Him again. He was here, in this hidden holy work of service He had entrusted to me.

The night before Jesus died, He prayed to the Father and said, "I glorified you on earth by finishing the work that you gave me to do" (John 17:4). The work the Father entrusted to the Son was hidden from the world. It didn't earn Jesus wealth or praise. It earned Him mockery, persecution, and death.

But it also earned Him the love of the poor, sick, and lame. He served them. He healed them. He died for them. He did what the Father asked Him to do. That brought glory to the Father and joy to the Son.

God has work for you too.

Whether that work is at home, at school, in the office, or at the store, whether the world sees your work or not, your work matters. God has entrusted work to you that is part of His plan for the world's salvation, work that will draw you and others closer to Him.

That work doesn't have to be impressive to be important. It just has to be done with love, integrity, and a desire to glorify God. That makes it a participation in Jesus' own work, bringing healing and joy to us and the world.

READING: JOHN 17:4

- How do you feel your work represents who you are? Is your work identity encroaching on your identity as God's daughter?
- If your work feels hidden and unimportant, and you are struggling with this, how can you offer this cross to Our Lord in prayer?

ALL ABOUT THE FOLLOWS AND LIKES

PURSUIT OF GLORY

I scanned the circular driveway in front of me. There she was, four cars back. I ran down the steps, away from the university's chapel and toward my roommate Maura's car.

"How was Mass?" she asked as I climbed in.

"Jesus was there," I replied. "But they sang that horrible song again."

"What makes the song horrible?" Maura asked, her quiet voice quieter than normal. "I've always liked it."

"Well, it starts with bad theology," I began. "Let me explain."

I was still explaining when we arrived home. "And that's why that song has no place in the liturgy," I concluded.

I waited for Maura to agree. Instead, without speaking, she slammed the door and walked inside.

I sat there, confused. What had I said? Why was she taking this so personally? When I finally went into the house, our other roommate, Jessica, stood waiting for me.

"Life isn't a blog, Emily," she said. "You can't talk to people like that."

"But I'm right!" I protested.

"I know you're right," Jessica replied. "But nobody cares how right you are if you're a jerk. What's happening to you? You never used to be like this before that stupid blog."

The "stupid blog" was something I had started a year earlier after I had moved to Ohio to study theology. By the second year of graduate school, it had become a major part of my life, and I loved it. I loved writing about the Faith. I loved engaging with other Catholics. And if I am being honest, I loved the follows, shares, and praise. Without realizing it, I had started chasing those follows, sharpening my tone, picking fights online, doing the things that got people talking. And it was paying off. My audience was growing quickly.

But Jessica was right. It was changing me, making me angrier, more argumentative, too sure of my own righteousness. I had plenty of knowledge but precious little wisdom. As so many of us do, I let my ego call the shots, never considering how my words might affect others. Spiritually speaking, I needed to grow up.

After that conversation, I realized I had a choice: keep blogging, reaping the accolades I craved, or step back until I had the spiritual maturity to share my opinions with humility and charity. I had to ask myself what we all have to ask ourselves eventually: Whom did I want to serve? Myself or God?

This is an ancient choice; Jesus Himself faced it in the desert.

"Again, the devil took him to a very high mountain and showed him all the kingdoms of the world and their splendor; and he said to him, 'All these I will give you, if you will fall down and worship me'" (Matthew 4:8–9).

Jesus answered by quoting the Scriptures: "Worship the Lord your God, and serve him only" (Matthew 4:10). Long before that, before the world began, Satan had faced the same choice but gave a different answer. "No, I will not serve," he had told God.

When it comes to our work, each of us faces this choice too. God or ourselves. Self-denial or self-seeking pleasure. Glory for Him or glory for us. Doing what's right, working with integrity, remembering obligations to others, and striving to serve the most vulnerable . . . or making compromises to advance, insisting the ends justify the means, ignoring obligations to others, and putting fame or profit before people.

The decision is ours. God won't force us to choose Him. But let us choose Him. Let us echo the words of Jesus in the desert and work in a way that glorifies Him.

READING: MATTHEW 4:8–10

- Are you tempted to chase prestige, praise, and affirmation in your work? Whose glory are you seeking? If it's not for God, take a long look at your motivations.
- Who in your life quietly pursues excellence and charity? What can you learn from his or her approach?

LET US
CHOOSE GOD.

EMILY STIMPSON CHAPMAN

SHARING OTHERS' STORIES

PURSUIT OF GOD

I was late. I had spent the morning writing a story for a Catholic newspaper about the pope's new encyclical and lost track of time. Now I had only a few minutes to get to the local university, where two of its donors, a husband and wife, waited. I was writing a profile about them for the school's magazine, and this was my one chance to talk with them in person.

By some small miracle, I arrived at the room where the donors waited, right as the noon Angelus bells rang out across campus.

I smiled, introduced myself, and turned on the tape recorder as I took a seat across the table from them.

Two hours later, I turned the recorder off. We chatted for fifteen more minutes, hugged goodbye, and promised to talk soon. When I had walked into that room, we were strangers. When I left, we were friends. They had trusted me with their story—of success and failure, of infertility and adoption, of wandering away from

God and returning to Him—and felt loved when I listened. Now I had to go home and do the hard work of sharing that story with others, honoring them by writing it well.

More than four years had passed since I had shut down my blog. I was still writing, but not essays or opinion pieces. Rather, I wrote stories about people, places, and problems in the world. I covered topics such as Church governance, Catholic education, and the struggles of the Church in China. Every week my editors assigned new stories to me, and every week my knowledge of Church and culture grew.

There was no food for my ego in this work. There was money to pay the bills, which I appreciated. And these stories reached more people than my blog ever did. But few who read what I wrote knew my name.

That was fine by me. I loved the freedom that came with not being part of the story. I loved getting to shine a light on truth, beauty, and goodness, helping others see how God moves in the world. I knew my work served others. It blessed others. But it blessed me the most. Every story I wrote taught me something. In different ways, each one helped me grow in wisdom and faith, drawing me closer to God as I wrote.

In Saint John's Gospel, Jesus warned, "Do not work for the food that perishes, but for the food that endures for eternal life, which the Son of Man will give you" (6:27). This seems impossible. Most of us must work for bread that perishes. Bills need to be paid. But Jesus isn't telling us to default on our mortgages. He's saying that if we want to grow closer to God, money cannot be the driving force behind our work. We need to work for something more, seeking His face and glory in all we do.

We do that when we pursue truth, goodness, and beauty because Jesus is Truth, Goodness, and Beauty.

For me, that meant writing true, good, and beautiful stories. For a teacher, it could mean sharing wisdom with students. For a small business owner, it might mean serving the common good with a product or service. For all of us, it means seeking to make the world a more graced place in the littlest of ways, from smiling at a difficult client to being patient with a disgruntled toddler.

When we pursue truth, beauty, and goodness, we pursue Christ. That pursuit changes our work, giving it life and bringing us joy.

READING: JOHN 6:27

- Pause to think over your daily life. Where do you experience truth, beauty, and goodness? Where can you bring truth, beauty, and goodness to those around you? Ask the Holy Spirit to illuminate this.
- Are you receiving the Blessed Sacrament at least weekly? Challenge yourself to receive this food that endures for eternal life once a week.

WORKING ONLY FOR TODAY

WRONGLY ORDERED PRIORITIES

"Dinner. Tonight. 6 pm. We're grilling. Can you come?"

I glanced at the message on my phone, quickly typed, "Maybe . . . I'll let you know," and went back to focusing on the computer screen in front of me.

It was only 11:00 a.m., but I had been staring at that screen for six hours and knew I would be staring at it for at least six hours more. I hadn't exercised. I hadn't showered either. The only time I had moved from my desk was to grab another cup of coffee.

I had done the same thing yesterday and the day before and every day before that for a month. My days had become a blur of researching, writing, and coffee. There wasn't time for anything else. Not for exercising. Not for cleaning or doing my laundry. And definitely not for taking friends up on dinner invitations.

"Maybe tonight," I whispered to myself. "If I just stay focused."

I stayed focused. But 6:00 p.m. came and went. Finally, at 7:00, I shut down the computer and drew a bath. A glass of wine, take-out sushi, and an episode of *Alias* followed. Then I went to bed, knowing I'd do it all again tomorrow.

I had brought the whole *Groundhog Day* mess on myself. A few months earlier, a publisher had proposed a project to me—a project with a lucrative check attached. It promised me enough money in the bank to live off of for months. And I needed that money. Or more accurately, I wanted that money. As a single woman, I wanted security. I wanted to know that even if all my other work dried up, I would be okay.

But money or no money, I had no business saying yes. I had already committed to two other big projects, plus I had all my normally scheduled writing. God was providing me with plenty of work. I had no reason to fear that would change. But like so many of us, I did fear. I didn't trust that He would provide. I didn't prayerfully discern which projects I should accept and which I should turn down. I just said yes to everything.

Now I was paying for that, scrambling to meet deadlines and dropping every other ball in my life. No matter how hard I tried, I couldn't keep up. Everything was out of balance.

That is what happens, though, when we make gods of something other than God. The result is chaos.

In my fear, I had left God out of my discernment about both daily tasks and future projects, making a god of financial security instead. I let that god order my days, forgetting Jesus' instructions in Matthew 6:34: "So do not worry about tomorrow, for tomorrow will bring worries of its own. Today's trouble is enough for today."

God has work for us to do each day, but He doesn't expect us to do it alone. He gives us grace to help—grace to work with love, grace to learn from our successes and failures, and grace to discern where our energy is most needed.

When we look to Him first and ask Him to guide us, balance follows. But when we look first to ourselves—our goals, plans, and fears—we miss out on the grace we need to order our work rightly. Even if we are checking items off our to-do lists, we can be mismanaging our time because they are *our* to-do lists, not His.

Invite God into your workday. Ask Him to provide strength and direction. Ask Him to make your efforts fruitful. His grace is more than sufficient, today and all days.

READING: MATTHEW 6:34

- Are you struggling with anxieties about provision? How is your balance? Do you find yourself struggling to say no to opportunities, constantly stressed?
- Does your to-do list include asking God what He wants of you for the week? Sit in quiet contemplation and ask Jesus to guide you to embrace what He wants for your time.

GOD'S GRACE IS
MORE THAN SUFFICIENT,
TODAY AND ALL DAYS.

EMILY STIMPSON CHAPMAN

REORDERING AND LETTING GO

RIGHTLY ORDERED PRIORITIES

"Are you going to say yes?"

I could barely hear my husband over our newborn's cries. "What are you talking about?" I asked, bouncing and patting the baby in my ongoing attempts to quiet him. "Say yes to what?"

"To the awards dinner in St. Louis. The speaking engagement. The one you mentioned last night."

Before I could answer, our two-year-old ran into the kitchen, where we stood talking. "I want a snack, Mama! Please!"

I wasn't sure who to answer first, my husband or our toddler. I split the difference by grabbing a package of fruit snacks from the cupboard and handing it to my son, while addressing my husband.

"I don't know," I told him. "I'm honored to be invited. And it's a great opportunity. I would sell a ton of books and get some helpful exposure. But how would we manage it with both boys? And with my book deadline. And . . . oh, Becket!"

As if to add emphasis to my point for me, my newborn had just vomited all over me.

"I would love to say yes, honey," I said, reaching for a burp cloth. "But something has to give, and I think it has to be speaking at conferences."

It had taken me two years and a second baby to admit that to myself. I wanted to do it all—write books, speak, be with my children. But the more speaking engagements I accepted, the more everything else fell apart.

Preparing talks ate into my already scarce writing time, while traveling to give those talks ate into time with my family. When I went to conferences alone, I missed deadlines and my boys. When they went with me, I missed sleep and struggled to form coherent sentences.

The more speaking engagements I accepted, the more miserable I became. Nobody was getting the best of me. It couldn't go on. Like all of us with too much on our plates, I had to let something go, putting what God had called me to do above what others (and sometimes I) wanted me to do.

For me, that meant my vocation as a wife and mother had to come first. My work as a writer had to come second. And speaking, which upended my ability to do everything else, had to go. It wasn't giving me life and helping me glorify God; it was robbing me of life and weakening my witness.

During His time on earth, Jesus modeled for us how to stay focused on what matters most. "My food is to do the will of him who sent me and to complete his work," He told the disciples (John 4:34). The Father's will for the Son was not easy. He called Jesus to proclaim the Kingdom of God when people wanted an earthly kingdom. Then He called Jesus to suffer and die for those who nailed Him to a cross.

The people who surrounded Jesus tried to dissuade Him from that work. They urged him to seek political power. They protested when He talked about suffering and dying. They tempted Him with worldly greatness and happiness. But Jesus would not be distracted. He put first the mission the Father had entrusted to Him, and that work fed His soul, strengthening Him as it glorified the Father.

God has entrusted a mission to each of us as well, giving us work in our families, the Church, and the world. Our work won't always be easy either, but when we prioritize rightly, staying focused on the people and tasks that matter most, we too will find food for our souls and bring glory to Him.

READING: JOHN 4:34

- Consider your priorities. Make a list. Now evaluate if they are simply crises du jour or truly how you want your life ordered. What is missing from the list?
- Saying no to something good can mean you are able to say yes to another good thing at a different time. If saying no is painful, whom can you ask in your life to walk through your obligations to discern which are bringing you closer to God?

PUTTING IN THE TIME

GRUDGING DISCERNMENT

Where is she? I stood at the front door, baby in arms, and scanned our street for the tenth time in ten minutes. I had three hours before a fundraising letter for one of my clients was due. If our sitter didn't get here soon, I wouldn't meet my deadline.

Just then, her car pulled into view. Moments later she was in the house, two lattes in hand.

The first words out of her mouth were an apology. "I'm sorry! The line was insane."

I took my coffee, reassured her everything was fine, and placed the baby in her arms while giving a few instructions about the toddler. I then raced up two floors to my attic office.

As I opened my laptop, a strong wave of discontent washed over me. I did not want to write this letter. What I wanted was to be downstairs with my babies . . . or editing my new book . . . or sharing something on Instagram. Heck, even cleaning my closets sounded more appealing.

But the fundraising letter had to be written. I had committed to doing it, and we needed the money. So I gritted my teeth, bent my head, and got to work.

I had been gritting my teeth a lot lately. With two babies already and a third on the way, my husband and I knew we needed to build up our savings account. So I had accepted a slew of boring but lucrative writing assignments. In the moment, I was never excited about them. There was always something more interesting to do.

I knew, though, that "interesting" is not always the most important thing. Helping provide for my family now and having enough in savings to take time off when our new daughter arrived mattered more than enjoying what I was doing in the moment.

At some point, for all of us, that's just how work goes. It doesn't feel particularly meaningful or important. It feels like a difficult, tedious means to an end. We grudgingly put in our time, tearing ourselves away from the five hundred other things we would rather be doing because of what we need to do—sometimes for the good of our family or ourselves, sometimes for the good of others or our community, sometimes just because we need to honor our word.

This is not necessarily a bad thing, though.

In Saint Mark's Gospel, Jesus compared remaining diligent in our work to remaining faithful to Him. He used an analogy of a man going on a journey who makes sure the work is taken care of in his absence and the workers stay alert. "Therefore, keep awake—for you do not know when the master of the house will come, in the evening, or at midnight, or at cockcrow, or at dawn" (13:35).

The comparison makes sense. With both work and our faith lives, we face the temptation to give up when things get tough.

Fortitude is the virtue that helps us avoid that mistake. It enables us to do the right thing, even when it is hard. We acquire that virtue through practice. The more we make good choices in the face of adversity, the easier making good choices gets.

Doing our duty at work, keeping our eyes focused on the good that that work makes possible, is one way we develop the virtue of fortitude. It trains us to remain faithful. It disciplines us, giving us the spiritual and mental strength to do hard things—for ourselves, others, and God.

Recognizing that truth changes our work, infusing even seemingly meaningless tasks with supernatural importance. Seen through the eyes of faith and done with love, no job you or I do is ever unimportant. Everything matters. Everything forms us. Everything helps us hold fast to Christ.

READING: MARK 13:33–35

- Becoming a saint by God's grace and growing in virtue doesn't happen in a vacuum. What is in front of you that is challenging you to grow in fortitude?
- Instead of going through the motions, where are you being called to approach a work situation or life challenge with a fresh perspective and with gratitude?

HOLD FAST
TO CHRIST.

EMILY STIMPSON CHAPMAN

WALKING THROUGH THE BEST DOOR

PRAYERFUL DISCERNMENT

"How do you do it all?" the message began. "Babies, work, keeping house—what's your secret?"

I stared at the message on my phone, a message from a stranger who followed me online. Then I looked up and glanced around.

Dishes were piled on the counter. Toy trucks were scattered about the dining room. My eleven-month-old was crawling around the kitchen, looking for Cheerios on the floor, while the two-year-old stood on a stool at the sink, splashing water everywhere as he "washed" my antique silver coffee pot. Our newborn daughter fussed in her bassinet in the corner, and since nobody's nap time had gone according to plan, I had no idea how I would meet my writing deadline for the day.

Do it all? I thought. *I feel like I can't do anything.*

Two months had passed since our daughter's birth, and I was struggling mightily to balance motherhood and work. I knew we couldn't make ends meet solely with what my husband earned teaching theology at a Catholic high school. But even with regular babysitting help, my writing felt impossibly difficult. Was God still asking me to do this? What did He want me to do?

I had asked that question years before, while working on my master's degree in theology. When I started graduate school, I thought I would eventually go on to earn my doctorate or get married and start a family. After two years of coursework, however, no husband was in sight, and I was burned out from my studies. I also needed money. After thinking and praying through my dilemma, I reached out to an editor who had read my old blog and offered me the chance to write for his publication: *Did he have work for me?*

He did. So did other editors. And before I knew it, I wrote for a living. The opportunities didn't stop. My need for income never stopped either. And although writing could be stressful, it was never boring. My interest in the work never waned. Neither did the good my work accomplished. Day after day, emails arrived from strangers who felt helped by what I wrote. Even when it was difficult, my work bore fruit.

Those are the markers for all of us discerning how God wants us to use our gifts and serve Him in the world: need, ability, desire, opportunities, fruit. And as we discern, we are reminded that when God wants us to do something, He makes it possible.

In Saint Luke's Gospel, Saint John the Baptist quoted the prophet Isaiah, "'Every valley shall be filled, and every mountain and hill shall be made low, and the crooked shall be made straight, and the rough ways made smooth'" (Luke 3:5). John was talking about the Messiah and how God would make His saving work possible.

Those words apply to our work, too, though. When God wants us to do something, He makes it possible. He makes crooked paths straight. He gives us the need, ability, desire, and opportunity to do the work, then makes our work fruitful. Good things happen. Words of encouragement come. So does satisfaction . . . and, occasionally, joy.

Remembering that is why I'm still writing, even with three small children. It is not easy, but somehow valleys get filled. Babies get loved, work gets done, bills get paid, and fruit is borne.

If you, too, are at a crossroads, look for the doors God is opening. Prayerfully consider your needs and/or your family's needs. Prayerfully consider your desires and abilities. Then walk through the door that seems best, looking for fruit as you go. If you are walking in the right direction, valleys will be filled and mountains laid low. What God calls us to do, He makes possible. Always.

READING: LUKE 3:5

- What feels impossible right now? What deadline, relationship, or prayer request? Turn to God and pour out your heart to Him.
- Which doors has God opened for you? Before crossing their thresholds, take courage in knowing you never walk alone. Ask Our Mother Mary to guide you as you follow His call.

EPILOGUE

BY JENNA GUIZAR

It has been quite a journey, this vulnerable look into relationships with Our Lord and others. He has done deep (sometimes painful), beautiful work in our hearts over the past fifty-two weeks. The well He has carved into our hearts is filling with Him, the Living Water. This journey has helped us remember He will heal, restore, and renew our hearts and our understanding of relationships, one drink at a time.

I know your journey has come such a long way, and I know there is more to do. But I rest assured in the truth that He is with you, that He is there for every single step you take in healing and navigating the many relationships in your life.

Your story will differ from each writer's in this devotional, but the universal truth is this: the Lord is with you. He is speaking to you through His Holy Word, and He brings greater insight, a deeper love, and more lasting healing than you could find anywhere else.

Let's keep drinking the Living Water. Here, the well never runs dry.

ABOUT THE
AUTHORS

Beth Davis is a lover of Jesus, a retired youth minister, and the director of ministry advancement for Blessed is She. She is passionate about teaching women how to develop an intimate relationship with Jesus and speaking hope to weary hearts. Her favorite things include being an aunt to her fab five niece and nephews, calling everyone "friend," and whatever book she's currently reading. She is a contributing author to *Maranatha: The Story of Our Savior*.

Megan Hjelmstad is a wife and hockey mom 24/7 and an Army Reservist in her "spare" time. She adores books, sleep, sunshine, and Colorado's great outdoors. Megan loves helping women discover their God-given dignity through Blessed is She's "The Well Mentorship" program. Megan is a contributing author to the children's devotional prayer book *Rise Up: Shining with Virtue* and *Maranatha: The Story of Our Savior*.

Nell O'Leary is the managing editor for Blessed is She. She is also an attorney-turned-writer, speaker, and editor, while tending to her husband and five children. She also facilitates Blessed is She community groups around the world, as she loves helping women find sisterhood. Her undergrad degree is in English from the University of Minnesota and her JD is from Ave Maria School of Law. She is an author of *Made New: 52 Devotions for Catholic Women.*

Bonnie Engstrom is a writer, baker, speaker, and homemaker. She lives with her husband and eight children in Illinois. Bonnie is the author of the children's book *Fulton Sheen and the Very Bad Week* and *61 Minutes to a Miracle*, which tells the story of her son's miracle that was approved by Pope Francis for the beatification of Venerable Fulton Sheen. She is also an author of *Mystery: Blessed Conversations Study on the Rosary.*

Sarah Erickson is an analyst for the Department of Justice. She earned her Master's in International Security from George Mason University and her Bachelor's in Politics from The Catholic University of America. Originally from Arizona, Sarah treasures iced oat milk lattes, mountain views, and Saint John Henry Newman. She resides in the Washington, DC, area with her cat, Regina. She is an author of *Dwell: Blessed Conversations Study on the Eucharist.*

Emily Stimpson Chapman is the author of more than a dozen books and studies for women, including *The Catholic Table: Finding Joy Where Food and Faith Meet* and *These Beautiful Bones: An Everyday Theology of the Body,* and is the general editor for the Formed in Christ high school textbook series. She lives in Pittsburgh with her husband and three children.

Jenna Guizar is a wife and mama in sunny Arizona. She loves spending time with her barber husband, her children, and dear friends. After she fell in love with the Lord through deep, faithful friends who prayed and spoke hope into her life, Blessed is She became her mission ground to help women love the Lord more and find deeper friendships with one another. She is an author of *Made New: 52 Devotions for Catholic Women*.

Susanna Spencer holds a master's in theology from the Franciscan University of Steubenville and is the theological editor of Blessed is She. She lives with her philosopher husband and four kids in Saint Paul, Minnesota. She loves reading theology, attending beautiful liturgies, cooking delicious food, and casually following baseball. She is the narrator for *Rise Up: Shining with Virtue* and *Marantha: The Story of Our Savior*.

Find out more about Blessed is She and our writers at *www.blessedisshe.net*.

BLESSED IS SHE

MADE NEW

52 DEVOTIONS
FOR CATHOLIC WOMEN

How would your life change if you were certain of your identity?
If you could know that Someone loves you, sees you,
and wants to be close to you—just as you are?
In this beautifully designed weekly devotional for women,
you're invited to soak in God's Word to embrace your
identity as a beloved woman made in God's image.

ISBN 978-1-4002-3024-2